Around the Shores of Lake Superior:
A Guide to Historic Sites

Around the Shores of Lake Superior:
A Guide to Historic Sites

Including a color tour map showing Lake Superior's historic sites

Margaret Beattie Bogue & Virginia A. Palmer

Published by
The University of Wisconsin Sea Grant College Program

Distributed through agreement by The University of Wisconsin Press

Library of Congress Catalog No. 79-65194.

ISBN 0-299-97013-2

Published by the University of Wisconsin Sea Grant College Program
with funding from the National Sea Grant Program, National Oceanic
and Atmospheric Administration, U. S. Department of Commerce, and
the State of Wisconsin.   WIS-SG-79-132

Produced and distributed in cooperation with the Great Lakes Sea
Grant Network.

ON THE COVER: *"Canoes in a Fog,"* painted by Frances Hopkins, an
Englishwoman who married a Hudson's Bay Company official.

–Photo courtesy of Glenbow Museum, Calgary, Alberta.

Contents

KEY TO SYMBOLS

P—picnicking   S—swimming

H—hiking $—admission charged

C—camping   *—included in the National
                       Register of Historic Places

F—fishing

B—boating   †—footnote symbol

ABOUT THE AUTHORS

Margaret Beattie Bogue and **Virginia A. Palmer** work for the University of Wisconsin-Extension's Department of Liberal Studies-History—Margaret, as a Professor in Madison and Virginia, as a Specialist in Milwaukee. Both have a great love for the history of the region and have written numerous publications. Of Lake Superior, they say: "We found the area intriguing—unique in its wildness and rich in its history. We wanted to know more about it and to share the information with fellow travelers." With support from the University of Wisconsin Sea Grant College Program, the authors began digging into the history of the region. Through dogged library research and contacts with local museum curators, government agencies, chambers of commerce, historical societies, departments of natural resources and "anybody who would talk to us," their detective work paid off in this guidebook. They are now working on a similar guide to historic sites on Lake Michigan.

STAFF FOR THIS BOOK

Project Coordinator: Linda Weimer
Publication Coordinator: Ann Cleeland
Design and Layout: Christine Kohler
Text Editors: Ann Cleeland, Pat Mitchell, Linda Weimer
Graphic Artists: Christine Kohler, Jana Fothergill, Nancy Cohen
Additional assistance provided by: Sandra Ingham, Jean Lang, Catherine Shinners, Warren Downs and Yvonne Peterson.

Captain Charles Winter and the steamer, BRUCE, early 1900s.

Acknowledgements

The authors are indebted to the many scholars whose studies touch upon Lake Superior's history. Their work provided much of the essential information for our guide. We are especially indebted to Grace Lee Nute, an outstanding scholar of the explorers, the French and British regimes, the fur trade, the missionaries, and Lake Superior, itself.

We would like to express our gratitude to a number of people who have read the manuscript, offered suggestions for changes and additions and pointed the way to additional resources for research. These include: Professor Elizabeth Arthur, Chairperson, Department of History, Lakehead University, Thunder Bay, Ontario; Professor George May, Department of History, Eastern Michigan University, Ypsilanti, Michigan; Professor David T. Halkola, Department of Social Sciences, Michigan Technological University, Houghton, Michigan; Professor James J. Talman, Department of History, University of Western Ontario, London, Ontario; Kenneth Bro, Advisory Services, University of Wisconsin Sea Grant College Program, Washburn, Wisconsin; Ryck Lydecker, Minnesota Marine Advisory Service, University of Minnesota, Duluth, Minnesota; George A. Talbot, Curator, and Myrna Williamson, Reference Assistant, Iconography Collection of the State Historical Society of Wisconsin.

The authors are especially indebted to the University of Wisconsin Sea Grant College Program, which funded the research of this guidebook, and to the staff of the Sea Grant Communications Office who edited, designed, and published this book.

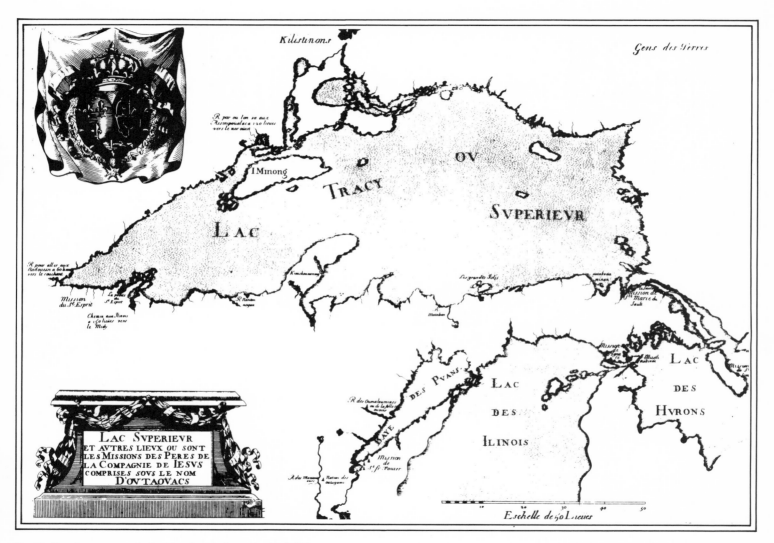

Facsimile of a map made by Jesuit missionaries in 1670.

"Though its waters are fresh and crystal, Superior is a sea."

—George Grant, 1872—Canadian Expedition

French explorers labeled it "superieur," the "uppermost" of the five Great Lakes. Although designated Lake Tracy for a time, in honor of the Governor General of New France, Superior became the lake's official name. It is a fitting one, since in surface area, Lake Superior is the largest body of fresh water in the world. The lake's clear blue waters and sheer rock cliffs also make Superior unique.

This strikingly beautiful lake and its shoreline have a long and venerable list of admirers. Radisson and Groseilliers, two of the earliest and most famous seventeenth century fur traders, traveled the lake and felt like "Caesars in the Wilderness."

Margaret Fuller, the pioneer American feminist, planned a trip to Lake Superior in 1843 ". . . to enter into that truly wild and free region." She wanted to canoe on the lake, camp under the stars and see the Pictured Rocks. Although her trip was cut short at Sault Ste. Marie, she did manage to descend the rapids of the St. Mary's River. She recorded: "I should like to have come down twenty times, that I might have had leisure to realize the pleasure."

Henry Schoolcraft, who accompanied Michigan's Territorial Governor, Lewis Cass, on an expedition to the sources of the Mississippi River in 1820, marveled at the scenery of Lake Superior's south shore. Entering the lake at the St. Mary's River, Schoolcraft wrote: "The entrance into Lake Superior was now in full view, presenting a scene of beauty and magnificence which is rarely surpassed, even amid the rugged scenery of the north." He described the Porcupine Mountains as "lofty and rugged," and the Apostle Islands as "a very beautiful and picturesque groupe."

Laurence Oliphant, a Canadian traveler, eulogized Lake Superior in 1855: "Of the wonderful series of lakes which extends halfway across the North American Continent, Lake Superior is by far the most interesting, not only to the scientific man on account of the singular geological formation of its shores, but to the traveler in search of magnificent scenery . . ."

Contemporary travelers continue to describe the lake with just as much eloquence and enthusiasm. Wisconsin Senator Gaylord Nelson describes Lake Superior as ". . . the same marvelously wild, breathtakingly beautiful lake seen by the first explorers who came to its shores nearly 300 years ago."

But a modern tour around Lake Superior provides more than a glimpse at nature's wonders. It also provides insight into the political, economic and cultural history of the region. How better to get a feeling for the fur trade than to visit the fine reconstruction of Fort William at Thunder Bay, Ontario? How better to sense the impact of the St. Lawrence Seaway than to see Duluth-Superior harbor, bustling with ships from all over the world?

This guidebook is meant to provide such experiences to Lake Superior travelers. Although the human history of the Lake Superior region is unique, there are common themes relating it to the history of the other Great Lakes.

Chief among these themes are the Indians, the first people to live in the area; the French explorers; the work of the Catholic and Protestant missionaries from the seventeenth through the nineteenth centuries; the fur traders; the international rivalries of the French and the British; and subsequent conflicts between the young United States and British Canada.

In the nineteenth and twentieth centuries, developmental themes have dominated Great Lakes history on both sides of the border: immigration, canal building, agriculture, commercial shipping, fishing, lumbering, mining, and industrialization. These developments led to a substantial mingling of Canadian and American people, capital, raw materials, ideas, institutions and technical knowledge.

Lake Superior's history reflects most, but not all, of these themes. As the westernmost of the five lakes, it experienced distinctive settlement and development patterns. Much of the region was technically frontier until well past the mid-nineteenth century and is still very sparsely populated. The topography, soils and length of the growing season make the lands lying around Lake Superior less suitable for agriculture than those located adjacent to the southern Great Lakes. But the area's wealth of fish, furs, forests and minerals and the availability of cheap water transportation significantly shaped its history.

Sections on these historical themes and on the impact of resource development on the region's character are scattered throughout the guide. Among the topics covered are the Chippewa people, missionaries, copper and iron mining, fur trade, shipping, lumbering, and the French-British conflict over territory.

For the most part, this guide is designed for people touring the Lake Superior shore. It contains information on 113 sites around the lake, beginning at Duluth-Superior and traveling north through Canada, back down through Sault Ste. Marie, and across Michigan and Wisconsin. Numbered entries are keyed to the color map that accompanies this guide.

Guidebooks tend to be selective and this one is no exception. The historic sites, museums and parks

The stockade and entrance gate to Fort William in Thunder Bay, Ontario.

described here are found, with few exceptions, close to the Lake Superior shore. This is because the authors have focused on the history of the area as it relates to the lake itself. Also included are other sites that are not in the immediate vicinity of the lakeshore, but have direct bearing on lake history.

The historical significance and location of each entry in the guide is briefly described. The authors have also written short histories of Lake Superior's major cities—Duluth, Superior, Thunder Bay and Sault Ste. Marie—to give the reader some idea of how these communities originated and what gives them their present vitality.

Guide listings also include national, provincial and state parks and national forests—sites offering camping and recreational opportunities that enhance the enjoyment of the Great Lakes environment. Also included are Indian reservations that reflect one segment of the history of the Indian people of Lake Superior.

The authors, editors and publisher hope that, no matter what experience you are seeking as you travel around Lake Superior, this guide will make your journey a far richer one.

Duluth~Superior

Entry 1

Duluth, Minnesota (circa 1871) showing Minnesota Point (center).

Originally, the home of the Sioux and Chippewa† Indians, the present site of the twin ports of Duluth, Minnesota and Superior, Wisconsin was known to the French voyageurs as Fond du Lac (bottom of the lake), an area including land on both the Wisconsin and Minnesota sides of St. Louis Bay as well as Minnesota Point.

The early history of Duluth-Superior is closely associated with the French explorers, fur traders and missionaries. Principal among them were

†Also referred to as Ojibwa and Ojibway (see "The Chippewa People," page 159).

Father Claude Allouez, who in 1655 built a mission adjacent to Allouez Bay; Radisson and Groseilliers, adventurous fur traders who came from Quebec in search of fortune in 1659-1660; and Daniel Greysolon, Sieur du Lhut, who came in 1679.

The latter, for whom Duluth is named, came on a mission to establish friendship between the French and the Chippewa and to encourage the Sioux to remain at peace with the Chippewa. Following a council meeting held not far from the present city of Duluth and the establishment of a fur trading post there, du Lhut pushed on to the Sioux Village at Mille Lacs Lake, hoping to further improve French-Sioux relations. Thereafter, the North West Company, the Hudson's Bay Company and finally John Jacob Astor's American Fur Company occupied fur trading posts in the Duluth area.

Permanent settlers came into the Duluth-Superior area during the land boom of the 1850s, shortly after the signing of the Treaty of La Pointe in 1854 and the completion of federal land surveys.

The dreams of southern land speculators led to the early development of the eastern part of Superior. The street names Corcoran, Walker and Breckenridge remind the visitor that Washington, D.C. banker William W. Corcoran, Mississippi Senator Robert J. Walker and Kentucky Congressman John D. Breckenridge had high hopes for profits from rising land values in northwestern Wisconsin. In contrast, Duluth had an even more modest beginning in the mid-1850s.

Ultimately Superior developed on level land with the familiar city grid pattern layout. But Duluth, situated between Lake Superior and a steeply rising bluff, developed all along the lake front with residential sections of the city nestled in the hills above.

Neither of the twin port cities grew much at all until well after the Civil War. When the eastern financier Jay Cooke visited Superior in 1868, he found it dilapidated in appearance with many empty houses. The town's Civil Wartime population of 700-800 had shrunk to 300. As for Duluth, it was a mere village with six or seven frame houses, a land office, a school and no hotel.

Ramshackle, rude and half-filled with Indians, the towns reminded Cooke of Sandusky, Toledo and Huron several decades earlier. He later said, "I felt sure that vast cities would grow up at Duluth and Superior."

The powerful banker became so enthused about the future of the Lake Superior region and the entire northwest that he threw his financial backing behind the two railroads. One was the Lake Superior and Mississippi Railroad, then in the process of construction from St. Paul to Duluth. The other was the Northern Pacific, planned to run from Portland, Oregon, to Lake Superior.

Both railroads had generous federal land grants. Before the financial collapse of Jay Cooke and Company in 1873, Cooke had established Duluth as the terminus of both roads and promoted the build-

When compared to the scene on p. 6, this 1888 photograph shows how amazingly fast Duluth grew in just 17 years.

ing of grain storage elevators, railroad docks, wharves, houses, stores, schools, churches and a bank.

The dream of Duluth as a major grain shipping point on a Mississippi River-Great Lakes route, which would be competitive with the interests in Chicago and Milwaukee, began to come true with the completion of the Lake Superior and Mississippi Railroad in 1871. Two million bushels of grain were shipped during the first year of operation.

From the perspective of hindsight, however, high hopes and meager results characterized Cooke's promotional efforts for Duluth from 1868-73. Save for the railroad construction that resulted in many jobs for the Duluth-Superior area, the economic potential for the twin ports awaited the end of hard times in the late seventies and the resumption of construction of the Northern Pacific Railroad.

Meanwhile Cooke's activities had further fanned the flames of rivalry between the twin ports. As Duluth forged ahead, boasting a population of 3,000 in 1870, Superior townspeople spoke of "Jay Cooke's Bubble" and called Duluth residents "cliff dwellers" and "hill climbers." Duluth residents responded by labeling Superior townspeople "swamp jumpers." The rivalry came to a climax with the efforts of the two towns to outbid each other as termination points for the Lake Superior and Mississippi, and North Pacific Railroads and in their fight over canal construction.

In 1870 developers hoped to cut a canal from the Duluth side of the harbor through Minnesota Point into the open lake. It became a live issue, with the backing of Jay Cooke. Some citizens of Superior, prominent among them a group of eastern investors with large real estate holdings there, opposed the project.

They feared that a completed canal, cut through Minnesota Point, would ruin the natural entrance to Superior's harbor by diverting the current of the St. Louis River. The proposed canal would definitely have made Duluth more accessible from Lake Superior for it would have lessened the distance from lake to port.

Undaunted by Superior opponents, Cooke and associates organized the Minnesota Canal and Harbor Improvement Company to make general harbor improvements, as well as to build the canal. To finance these improvements, Cooke had a Duluth Harbor bill introduced in Congress seeking a federal land grant of 500,000 acres. The measure failed to pass. Canal construction went forward nevertheless.

Begun in 1870, the canal was completed in 1871 under dramatic circumstances. The people of Superior decided to put a stop to the project and enlisted the aid of the U.S. War Department. In June 1871, they secured a federal court injunction to stop canal construction. The Duluth canal builders learned in advance that the injunction would be delivered in five days by an Army officer en route from Leavenworth, Kansas. Feverish digging and dredging paid off. By the time the officer got to Duluth with the legal papers, the canal was an accomplished fact.

To quiet ill feeling in Superior, the town of Duluth raised $100,000 to build a dike across the bay to prevent the St. Louis River from being diverted through the canal. The dike was never satisfactory—bit by bit it disappeared from natural and unnatural causes until in 1887, the U. S. government, assuming operation of the harbor, removed what was left. In 1898 the U.S. Army began improvements on the canal, which was eventually widened to 300 feet.

Although Duluth incorporated as a town in 1870, it went back to village status during the economically depressed years of the 1870s, then reincorporated as a town in 1887. On the Superior side, a single incorporated municipality took form in 1889 comprised of the earlier settlement of the 1850s—in what is now the eastern part of Superior—and West and South Superior.

Much of the economic growth and prosperity of Duluth-Superior in the late nineteenth century stemmed from lumbering. In the 1880s the twin ports prospered, as Michigan and Maine lumbermen moved westward from their cutover forests to join midwestern timber barons in harvesting the great stands of white pine in the Lake Superior region.

As the Northern Pacific reached completion in the 1880s and the Great Northern Railroad in the next decade, settlers pushed into the wheat lands of the U.S. and Canada. Wheat shipments, along with the milling and shipping of lumber, spurred the economic growth of the port cities.

Brown's lumber camp and train at Brule, Wisconsin in 1893.

Mineral explorations of the northern Minnesota Vermilion range in the mid-seventies, followed by mining in the 1880s and the opening of the Mesabi range in 1892, added new economic activity at a time when the days of the vast lumbering industry were numbered.

After World War II, the development of a commercially feasible process for handling low grade taconite ores gave new life to the iron mining areas of Minnesota and to the twin port cities, as did the piping of oil into the ports from Alberta oil fields and the opening of the St. Lawrence Seaway.

Transportation, communication, utility, health and educational services are Duluth-Superior's major employers. The half-dozen largest manufacturing plants produce frozen foods, tools, wood products, insulation and hydraulic equipment.

Duluth-Superior has a particularly fine deep-water harbor with a shared waterfront that includes 50 docks. The two ports boast one of the tallest grain elevators in the United States; the largest iron ore docks in the United States (established by the Great Northern Railroad in 1899); and a terminal for one of the longest oil pipeline systems in the Western Hemisphere, owned by the Lakehead Pipe Line Company, Inc.

The newest waterfront facility on Allouez Bay is a pellet loading dock and storage facility, which was built by the Burlington Northern Railroad. The Burlington Northern's new transshipment terminal handles 20 million tons of low sulphur coal from Montana each year. Most of it goes to coal-burning power plants in the East.

In September 1977 Cargil, Inc. dedicated a new terminal at Duluth, increasing the port's handling capacity to 75 million bushels of grain annually. Grain at a rate of 140,000 bushels per hour can be loaded onto ships. Shipments of iron ore, coal, grain and Canadian crude oil place Duluth-Superior, the western terminal of the St. Lawrence Seaway, second only to the port of New York in total tonnage handled in the U.S.

Visiting Duluth-Superior are U.S. and Canadian ships trading on the Great Lakes, as well as overseas ships using the St. Lawrence Seaway. A Minnesota-Wisconsin commission is now studying the possibility of merging the ports of Duluth and Superior. The merger idea harks back to Jay Cooke's efforts of more than a century ago to secure a strip of land from Wisconsin which would unite the twin ports.

In Duluth harbor, the German cargo ship, SIRIUS, loads coal bound for England.

Brimming with sightseers, the only whaleback passenger ship, CHRISTOPHER COLUMBUS, passes beneath a Milwaukee drawbridge.

Duluth and Superior also share the history of Alexander McDougall's shipbuilding enterprise. The American Steel Barge Company, which began in Duluth, was moved to expanded facilities in Superior in 1890. The company was building ships called "whalebacks," designed by Captain Alexander McDougall.

McDougall described his unique invention as "a boat with a floating bottom designed to carry the least water, a round top so water does not stay on board, and a spoon-shaped bow to best follow the line of strain." The ships had cigar-shaped hulls, with tapered ends that were sometimes said to resemble a pig's snout. The ships were cheap and easy to build. Their streamlined design resulted in a saving of fuel and their unobstructed holds were made for speed in loading.

Thirty-nine whalebacks were launched by 1899 at the ports of Duluth and Superior. However, by this time their disadvantages — especially the way they rolled during stormy weather — were becoming as apparent as their advantages, and more modern freighters began to replace the whalebacks in popularity. McDougall's one passenger whaleback, the CHRISTOPHER COLUMBUS, continued to carry passengers between Milwaukee and Chicago until 1931. It had been built for the Goodrich Transit Company at the time of the World's Columbian Exposition in 1893 (see "Lake Superior's Ships," page 21).

SUPERIOR, WISCONSIN

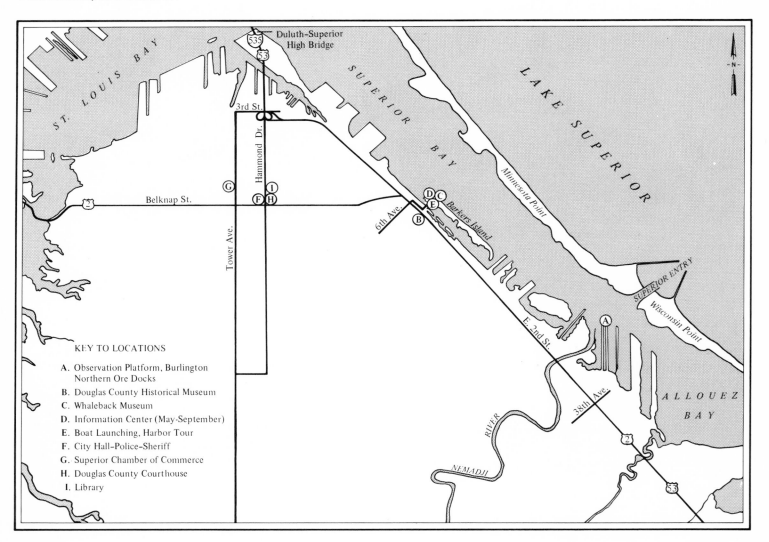

535 Duluth-Superior
High Bridge
53

ST. LOUIS BAY

SUPERIOR BAY

LAKE SUPERIOR

3rd St.

Hammond Dr.

G   I
F H

Belknap St.

Tower Ave.

D C
E   *Barkers Island*
B

6th Ave.

Minnesota Point

SUPERIOR ENTRY

Wisconsin Point

E. 2nd St.

A

38th Ave.

ALLOUEZ BAY

RIVER

NEMADJI

53

KEY TO LOCATIONS

A. Observation Platform, Burlington
Northern Ore Docks
B. Douglas County Historical Museum
C. Whaleback Museum
D. Information Center (May-September)
E. Boat Launching, Harbor Tour
F. City Hall-Police-Sheriff
G. Superior Chamber of Commerce
H. Douglas County Courthouse
 I. Library

SUPERIOR SITES OF INTEREST

Observation platform for the Burlington Northern ore docks is at 36th Avenue East and the end of First Street. These docks are so large that 12 ships can be loaded at one time.

The Douglas County Historical Museum, 906 East Second Street (also Hy 2, across the street from Barker's Island). The museum is headquartered in a 42-room mansion built by Martin Pattison in 1889. After the death of the lumber magnate, the house became an orphanage and was donated to the Maritime Society in 1963. Open year-round, closed Mondays.

Whaleback Museum. Today, only one whaleback freighter survives—the METEOR.* Donated to the Head of the Lakes Maritime Society in 1972, the ship was brought back to Superior, less than a mile from where it was built in 1896.

Used as an ore carrier until 1925, the METEOR was originally named FRANK ROCKEFELLER for a director of the American Steel Barge Company. The freighter carried grain, sand and automobiles until it ran aground in 1942. After repairs, it was renamed METEOR by the new owners, Cleveland Tankers, Inc. and commissioned to carry 42,000 barrels of oil with a crew of 29.

Now retired, the ship has been placed on display at Barker's Island, connected by a bridge to Hy 2. Open to the public daily in summer as a marine museum. For information, call 715/392-5742 or write Whaleback, Box 178, Superior, Wisconsin 54880. ($)

Duluth-Superior Harbor Tour. Two excursion boats, the VISTA QUEEN and the VISTA KING leave from Superior at Barker's Island and from Duluth at the Seaway Excursion dock behind the Arena, June-September. ($)

In summer, 40,000 visitors tour the whaleback freighter, METEOR, now a museum.

DULUTH, MINNESOTA

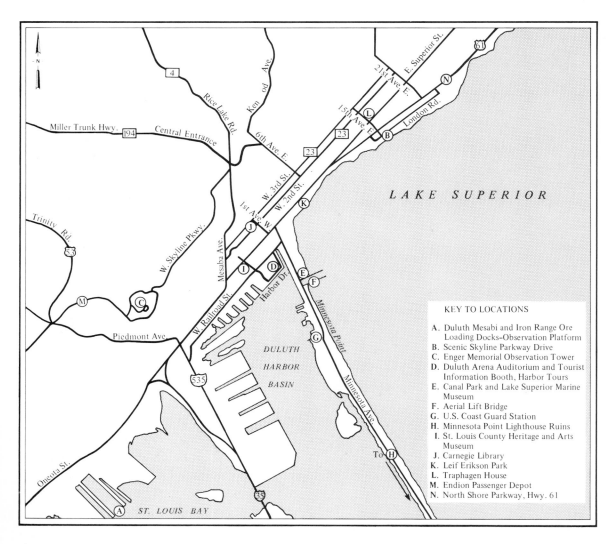

LAKE SUPERIOR

DULUTH HARBOR BASIN

ST. LOUIS BAY

KEY TO LOCATIONS

A. Duluth Mesabi and Iron Range Ore Loading Docks–Observation Platform
B. Scenic Skyline Parkway Drive
C. Enger Memorial Observation Tower
D. Duluth Arena Auditorium and Tourist Information Booth, Harbor Tours
E. Canal Park and Lake Superior Marine Museum
F. Aerial Lift Bridge
G. U.S. Coast Guard Station
H. Minnesota Point Lighthouse Ruins
I. St. Louis County Heritage and Arts Museum
J. Carnegie Library
K. Leif Erikson Park
L. Traphagen House
M. Endion Passenger Depot
N. North Shore Parkway, Hwy. 61

DULUTH SITES OF INTEREST

Duluth Mesabi and Iron range ore loading docks-observation platform, at the end of Frontage Road (reached by 46th Avenue West, foot of 35th Avenue West and Superior Street). Built in 1915, these ore docks stretch 2,304 feet into Lake Superior.

Scenic Skyline Parkway Drive, 27 miles long, connects Hy 39 on the southwest side of Duluth with Hy 61 on the northeast side and Jay Cooke State Park. The drive, 450 feet above the present Lake Superior shoreline, is the prehistoric shoreline of glacial Lake Duluth.

Enger Memorial Observation Tower on West 16th Avenue, offers a panoramic view of the St. Louis River and Duluth's inner harbor.

Lake Superior Marine Museum, Canal Park. The U.S. Army Corps of Engineers and a citizen's advisory committee developed this museum to present the history and growth of Upper Great Lakes shipping. The visitors' center, shaped like a ship's bridge, contains many artifacts of Lake Superior shipping and diving, and affords a panoramic view of harbor traffic. A restored 36-foot U.S. Coast Guard surfboat is also on the grounds. Open daily, year-round.

Aerial lift bridge* in Canal Park on Lake Avenue South. When the ship canal was dug in 1871, ferry or footbridge provided the only means of crossing over to Minnesota Point, except in wintertime when

Enger Memorial Observation Tower.

Aerial lift bridge, Duluth.

the ice was safe to cross. The aerial bridge spanning the ship canal at Duluth Harbor was originally designed by Thomas F. McGilvray in 1905 to withstand severe winter gales. The bridge closely resembled one in Rouen, France. It had a suspended gondola car which carried passengers and automobiles from one end to the other. In 1929 this was converted to a lift span bridge designed by C.P.A. Turner. Upon the approach of a ship the span can rise 138 feet above the water in 55 seconds.

U.S. Coast Guard Station on Minnesota Avenue. The Coast Guard Cutter WOODRUSH, moored 12 blocks south of the aerial bridge on the bay side of Minnesota Avenue, is open to visitors weekend afternoons in summer.

Minnesota Point Lighthouse*, at the east end of Minnesota Point. Although this lighthouse, built in 1858, operated for only 20 years, the brick column which protected the lighthouse still stands. A marker on the column indicates that it is point zero from which surveys of Lake Superior began. The lenses, made in France, are used in the west pierhead light today. The visitor can walk two miles out to the site from the mainland or view it by boat from Duluth Harbor.

Together, Minnesota Point and Wisconsin Point are believed to form the largest freshwater sandbar in the world—a distance of nine miles from one end to the other. The St. Louis and Nemadji Rivers keep the natural outlet of the Superior entry canal open for shipping.

St. Louis County Heritage and Arts Museum*, 506 West Michigan. The Burlington Northern Railroad built this structure in 1892 to serve as the Duluth Union Depot. Designed in Norman French style by the Boston firm of Peabody and Stearns, the building became a cultural center after the Burlington Northern discontinued passenger service.

The Michigan Street and mezzanine levels house the Duluth Art Institute, the Duluth Playhouse and exhibits on immigrants, lumbering and logging assembled by the St. Louis County Historical Society. At track level, next to the Amtrak depot, the visitor can tour the Lake Superior Museum of Transportation and Industry, opened in 1977. It is filled with dozens of old railroad cars and engines, old ore carriers, snow removal engines and passenger cars. The A. W. Chisholm Museum exhibits a Minnesota Redwood Habitat in the former depot baggage room. The building is open daily and Sunday afternoons in summer, weekends in winter. ($)

Carnegie Library, 1st Avenue West and 2nd Street. Louis C. Tiffany designed two windows in this building that depict the area's history. Adolph F. Rudolf, a local architect, designed the building, built in 1902.

Leif Erickson Park, London Road and 10th Avenue East. The park contains a replica of ships used by the Vikings, who were said to have visited America in 977 A.D. This replica sailed from Bergen, Norway to Duluth in 1926.

Oliver G. Traphagen House (Redstone)*, 1509-1511 East Superior Street. Oliver G. Traphagen, a leading architect in Duluth's development, designed many

Quiet reigns in the Carnegie Library, 1902.

The St. Louis County Heritage and Arts Museum is housed in the old Duluth railway depot.

downtown businesses as well as large dwellings and townhouses. He designed Redstone and had it built in 1892 as a home for his own family—a double residence with two separate entrances. All of the major rooms contained fireplaces. Today the large sandstone building has been made into apartments. Traphagen left Duluth in 1897 because of illness in his family and died in San Francisco in 1932.

Endion Passenger Depot*, 1504 South Street (at 15th Avenue East). This was the first passenger stop after 1st Avenue East on the Duluth, Mesabi and Iron Range Railroad. The railroad built the depot in 1899. The architects, Gerhard A. Tenbusch and I. Vernon Hill of Duluth, used sandstone and pressed brick in a Romanesque style. Endion was once a separate community, but is now part of Duluth.

North Shore Parkway, 190 miles long, connects with the Canadian border. The parkway offers the traveler unusually fine views of the lake.

LAKE SUPERIOR'S SHIPS

Duluth Harbor, 1880.

For more than three centuries, Canadians and Americans have traversed the deep, cold waters of Lake Superior. In that time, the most enduring craft has been the birchbark canoe. Developed by the Algonquian Indians, its seaworthiness was severely tested by the lake's sudden storms and turbulent waters. The Indians and later, explorers, missionaries and voyageurs were well served by the small canoe. The fur traders adapted the size of the birchbark canoe to suit their needs: the Montreal canoe was the largest , carrying a crew of six to 12; the canot du nord or north canoe was somewhat smaller; and the "bastard" canoe was somewhere between the Indian birchbark canoe and the canot du nord in size. Today, visitors at Fort William in Thunder Bay can watch skilled craftsmen build birchbark canoes with the same materials used back in the fur trading era (see Thunder Bay, entry 26).

In the late eighteenth century when canoes proved too small for the needs of the fur trade and sailships were few in number, the bateau and the mackinaw boat came into use on Lake Superior. The bateau was a long boat, made of wood—usually red cedar. It had high pointed ends and a flat bottom. Designed for use in deep water, but not for portaging, it carried a heavier load than a canoe and sailed under many different wind conditions. The mackinaw boat was also flat-bottomed and had rounded ends, a very sturdy frame, rudder and mast. It could sail 60 to 70 miles per day with the right wind conditions. The mackinaw boat was described as "a cross between a dory and a mud-scow, having something of the shape of the former and something of the clumsiness of the latter." When conditions permitted, canoes, bateaux, and mackinaw boats all used sails on Lake Superior; on still days, oars propelled these boats through the deep lake waters.

Decked sailing ships first appeared on Lake Superior in the eighteenth century. The earliest was the LA RONDE, built in the 1730s at Pointe aux Pins and used for copper mining ventures along the southern shore. Later in the century, Alexander Henry (see Victoria, entry 93) had a barge and a 40-ton sloop built, also for use in copper mining ventures along the southern and northeastern shores of Lake Superior.

From the 1700s on into the 1800s, sailing ships crossed Lake Superior, serving the needs of the fur-trading companies—the North West Company, the Hudson's Bay Company and the American Fur Company. In the 1830s the latter two trading firms added several sailing ships to their fleets to serve their expanding fishing enterprises. By the mid 1840s, 12 such ships sailed from port to port on Lake Superior, carrying prospectors, miners, soldiers, missionaries, and supplies. But the rapids of the St. Mary's River at Sault Ste. Marie severely restricted their movement, confining them primarily to Lake Superior. Ships that tried to run the rapids frequently were wrecked. At times both sailing ships and steamboats were hauled around the rapids on rollers at great expense and effort. This problem was solved with the completion of the American Canal in 1855. The canal opened a whole new era in shipping and fostered the exploitation of the region's natural resources. Lake Superior became a major highway between its hinterland and cities on the lower Great Lakes.

The first steamboat appeared on Lake Superior in 1841. A sidewheeler, it was soon followed by steamboats driven by screw propellers. At first, wood—secured from fuel stations along the shore—powered the ships, but by the 1860s, coal began to be used. The steamers shared the lake with wooden sailing ships, whose popularity peaked in the mid-1860s. These gradually lost out to the steam-propelled vessels made of iron and steel.

A new kind of lake transport emerged in the 1860s with steam barges and "tows"—a cheap method for moving large cargoes of heavy bulky freight. Old sailing vessels were adapted for use in these tows. They became especially important in transporting logs and lumber during the heyday of lumbering on Lake Superior in the late nineteenth century.

In 1889 a very special vessel came into being on Lake Superior—the whaleback. This ore carrier, which resembled a floating steel cigar, met the needs of the developing iron ore industry of Minnesota. It provided a cheap, efficient way to transport ore to the lower lakes. Captain Alexander McDougall developed the whaleback, a forerunner of the modern ore carrier. McDougall had spent his early life in the shipbuilding town of Collingwood, Ontario. For many years he worked on Lake Superior ships, first as a second mate and finally as a ship captain. He later designed the whaleback, 46 of which were built by the American Steel Barge Company between 1889 and 1898. Today, visitors to Superior can tour the only remaining whaleback ship—the METEOR—now a marine museum (see Duluth-Superior, entry 1).

The first modern bulk freighter on the Great Lakes was the iron steamer, OKONO, launched at Cleveland in 1882. Since then, bulk carriers have been steadily improving in design to provide cheaper and more efficient transportation. Today's freighters are often completely automated. These are self-unloading ships with automated dockside equipment. Duluth-Superior (see entry 1) and Thunder Bay (see entry 26) offer excellent

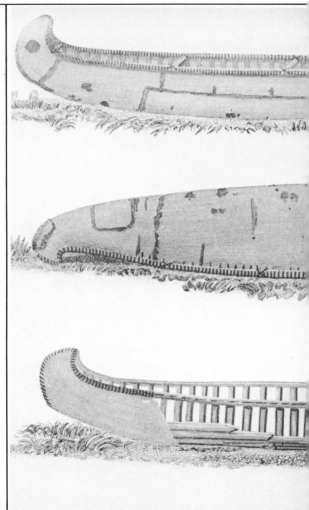

Chippewa birchbark canoes.

opportunities to observe these automated loading and unloading operations. Principal cargoes now outbound from Superior's port cities are iron ore, grain, and oil; inbound cargoes include coal, automobiles and a wide variety of machinery and equipment. Observing these highly efficient loading and unloading operations in Duluth, it is difficult to imagine the sight of the first cargo of commercial coal being unloaded there in wheelbarrows in 1871.

Great changes have characterized the history of shipping on the Great Lakes, especially since World War II. Passenger boats that regularly plied Lake Superior, connecting Duluth-Superior, Thunder Bay and Sault Ste. Marie with the ports of the lower lakes, were a significant part of the lake's traffic well into the twentieth century. Steamships carried passengers, mail and freight in the post Civil War years; they developed as part and parcel of the nineteenth century passenger service of the Canadian and American railroad systems. Early railroad advertisements described the scenic wonders of a cruise on the Great Lakes and promoted this elegant way of traveling across the country. The advent of the automobile, an excellent road system and air travel eroded the appeal of the more relaxed excursion by rail and boat. Consequently, these regular passenger ships, along with the lake cruise ships, disappeared after World War II.

Also following World War II came the virtual disappearance of the U.S. package fleet from the lakes. In 1970 most of the 44 ships, catagorized as domestic general cargo freighters, were relatively new Canadian vessels. The decline in cargo freighters of American registry can be attributed to competition from the American trucking industry and airlines.

Most significant of all post-World War II shipping changes was the opening of the St. Lawrence Seaway in 1959. This transformed Great Lakes ports into international ports, capable of handling large oceangoing vessels. Vessels from around the world are now a familiar sight at Sault Ste. Marie, Duluth-Superior and Thunder Bay. The captain's dinner aboard a Russian grain carrier has become an important social event to those Duluth-Superior townspeople lucky enough to be invited.

In 1970 the domestic U.S. and Canadian Great Lakes fleet totalled 454 vessels in all categories: dry bulk carriers, self unloaders, tankers, crane vessels, and package freighters. The largest category was the dry bulk carrier. There were 266 of these in 1970; they principally handled iron ore and grain. The oceangoing Great Lakes Seaway fleet included 296 American, Canadian and foreign vessels—partly bulk carriers and partly general cargo ships. Much of the Great Lakes fleet was relatively old in 1970; 40 percent of all the vessels had been built between 1890 and 1929.

What does the future hold for the Great Lakes domestic fleet? Experts predict that the long-range trend will be toward larger, deeper-draft vessels if the canals, locks, and harbor facilities in the St. Lawrence Seaway System can be expanded and enlarged to make this possible. At present, the largest ships in the Great Lakes fleet are 1,000-foot ore carriers, which just barely fit through the locks at Sault Ste. Marie and are much too large to fit through the locks in the St. Lawrence Seaway.

In the future the bulk carrier fleet will probably continue the trend toward fewer, larger, swifter and more automated carriers; the tanker fleet is expected to remain fairly constant. Eighty percent of the overseas fleet will probably need to be replaced soon. Experts see adaptability and flexibility as major requirements for future Great Lakes shipping fleets to handle an expanding volume of overseas cargo.

For more information on the history of shipping on Lake Superior, visitors should stop at the Lake Superior Marine Museum at Duluth (see Duluth-Superior entry 1).

The ore carrier, CLIFFS VICTORY, entering Duluth Harbor.

2. FOND DU LAC RESERVATION

[Hy 2 or 210]

Twenty miles west of Duluth lies the Fond du Lac Reservation for Chippewa Indians, which covers 40,000 acres. It is one of six Chippewa reservations in Minnesota that are home to the Minnesota Chippewa Tribe as organized under the Indian Reorganization Act of 1934. The natural resources of the reservation include timber, sand, gravel and peat. Tribal income derives chiefly from forestry and farming and there are a number of commercial and industrial businesses in the reservation communities. About 680 Indians reside on or adjacent to the reservation.

3. JAY COOKE STATE PARK

[Southwest of Duluth with access from Hy 210, (P-H-C-F)]

Established in 1915 when administrators of Jay Cooke's estate gave the state of Minnesota 2,000 acres, the park honors Cooke's contributions in promoting and developing the city of Duluth (see entry 1).

A trail which was once the "Grand Portage of the St. Louis"* may still be seen in the park near Hy 39,

about four miles northeast of today's campground. The portage, made necessary by the rapids and falls of the St. Louis River, was used by the North West Company until the end of the War of 1812 and later was used by the American Fur Company.

4. TWO HARBORS

[Hy 61]

The first of Minnesota's iron ore ports, Two Harbors earned its name from the harbors on Burlington and Agate Bays, although only the Agate Bay Harbor is commercially developed. This town served as the 1884 terminus of the Duluth and Iron Range Railroad, which in the summer of that year carried the first iron ore shipment from the mining boom town of Tower in the Vermilion range—ten cars loaded with 220 tons of ore. By 1887 annual shipments from Tower to Two Harbors rose to 400,000 tons.

Lake County Historical Museum occupies the brick building built in 1907 as the railroad office and depot. It contains displays on railroading, logging, iron mining and fishing. Open from May-October.

Van Haven Park affords a good view of the loading of iron ore carriers. The visitor can also watch the tugboat EDNA G.* at work. The tug, named for the daughter of a president of the D & IR Railroad, docks at the south end of Poplar Street on Agate Bay. The Cleveland Ship Building Company built the tug in 1896 for the Duluth and Iron Range Railroad.

The EDNA G. guides ore carriers to the docks at Two Harbors and is believed to be the last steam-powered, hand-fired, coal-burning tugboat assigned an operating license on the Great Lakes. It has been included on the National Register of Historic Places as an important example of earlier Great Lakes vessels.

5. GOOSEBERRY FALLS STATE PARK
[Hy 61, (P-H-C-F)]

Before the state of Minnesota acquired this park site in 1933, the area had been extensively logged. Huge white pine stumps remain in the park and bear witness to this past. Log rafts were floated from a landing on the present site of the picnic grounds.

Gooseberry Falls.

At least five waterfalls of the Gooseberry River, two more than 30 feet high, carry its water into Lake Superior. Above the lake shore rise cliffs at least 300 feet high, offering a vantage point for a magnificent view of the lake. Hiking trails lead to Lower and Upper Falls of the Gooseberry River, which takes its name from one of two explorers who were probably the first white men in this area. Medard Chouart, Sieur des Groseilliers and Pierre Esprit Radisson, his brother-in-law, built a cabin on Chequamegon Bay in 1659, from which they explored much of the north shore of Lake Superior (see entry 103). When the British came, they adopted place names from early maps but altered the spellings to forms that were more familiar. Groseilliers and Radisson became Gooseberries and Radishes, and thus the Gooseberry River acquired its name.

6. SPLIT ROCK STATE PARK
[Hy 61, (P-H)]

The Minnesota Territorial Legislature ignored requests in 1854 and later for funds to build a lighthouse here. Twenty-six vessels sank or became stranded near the bluff before funds were at last appropriated in 1905. An octagonal lighthouse 54 feet high was completed in 1910. The light was visible for 23 miles and the foghorn could be heard five miles away.

Before the state highway extended to Split Rock in 1924, the first visitors to the light came by boat. Split Rock lighthouse* is now the most visited lighthouse on the Great Lakes and is the unofficial

Split Rock Lighthouse.

symbol of the north shore of Lake Superior. After the light was automated in 1961, the land and a complex of ten buildings were donated to the state for a park, which was dedicated in 1971.

The Minnesota Historical Society operates the lighthouse site and offers tours which relate the history of this former U.S. Coast Guard Station and an explanation of how the lens operates. The Society is now restoring the fog signal house and the keeper's residence. When completed, these will also be open for tours. Open weekends in May, and daily, Memorial Day through October 15. Picnic facilities and hiking trails extend down to the shore.

7. BEAVER BAY

[Hy 61]

Although historians are unsure of the date of its original white settlement, Beaver Bay is believed to have been one of the earliest settlements on Lake Superior's north shore. A group of German immigrants from Ohio reached this spot in 1856 and decided to settle there. Although they had expected to take up farming, the Germans found the establishment of a sawmill more profitable. The mill paved the way for friendly relations with the area's Chippewa Indians, for whom it provided employment.

8. SILVER BAY

[Hy 61]

Silver Bay is an incorporated village built in 1955 for employees of the Reserve Mining Company and their families. In Silver Bay is the world's first large-scale taconite pellet producing plant, the E. W. Davis works. Although taconite was discovered in 1871, it took many years of research by Dr. Davis and others before taconite could be utilized for commercial purposes. When it became apparent that the supply of natural iron ore would soon be depleted in Minnesota, the use of taconite, a lower grade ore, became more imperative.

Since it is only 20-35 percent iron, the crude ore must be crushed into a fine powder and the dust-sized grains combined into pellets for shipping. Two movable boat loaders transfer the pellets from storage bins to ore carriers at the rate of 3,000 tons per hour.

In Silver Bay's natural harbor, a harbor of refuge has been created for the carriers which transport the pellets to steel mills on the lower lakes. Breakwaters have been built from shore to Pellet and Beaver Islands. The latter island boasts rare plant species and a herring gull colony.

Silver Bay and the Reserve Mining Company have recently been at the center of the most bitter environmental controversy yet known in the Lake Superior region. At issue has been Reserve's dumping of taconite tailings into Lake Superior.

Since the plant opened in 1957, 275 million tons of tailings have been dumped into the lake. In 1969, the state of Minnesota took Reserve Mining to court to put a stop to this dumping and in 1973, a federal judge ordered the company to switch to a land disposal site. He cited the health hazard posed to Min-

Reserve Mining Company plant at Silver Bay.

nesota north shore residents by the waterborne wastes. Reserve is scheduled to begin dumping the tailings on land by 1980.

The Reserve Mining court case was a classic one, pitting environmental concerns against economic ones. On the one hand were concerns over the water quality of Lake Superior—the largest and purest of the Great Lakes. On the other were the 3,200

workers in Silver Bay who depend on the Reserve plant for their livelihoods, and the Reserve operation itself, which processes almost 20 percent of the nation's raw iron ore into taconite pellets for making steel.

St. Mary's Roman Catholic Church in Silver Bay has a unique altar and baptismal font which were made especially for this church from a 5,000-pound block of polished taconite.

9.   BAPTISM RIVER STATE PARK

[Hy 61, (P-H-F)]

This park of outstanding beauty includes one of the highest waterfalls in the state. On the Lake Superior shore is a 170-foot wall of rock known as Shovel Point.

10.   CARIBOU FALLS STATE PARK

[Hy 61, (P-H-F)]

Although they are now seldom seen, caribou were once a common sight in northern Minnesota. The falls and forest scenery make this a delightful picnicking site.

11. TACONITE HARBOR

[Hy 61]

Officials of the Erie Mining Company built this town just a few years after Silver Bay. Taconite pellets shipped here are processed at the company's taconite processing plant at Hoyt Lakes about 64 miles west. An observation stand offers a view of the ship loading operations.

An 1873 view of the entrance to Baptism Bay.

12. SUPERIOR NATIONAL FOREST
[Off Hy 61, (P-H-C-F-B-S)]

The U.S. Department of Agriculture established the Superior National Forest in 1909 under the National Forest Service. Today the Superior Forest covers over two million acres, the largest national forest east of the Mississippi River.

Originally, the land belonged to the Chippewa Indians, and it has been traveled by voyageurs, miners and lumberjacks. The forest's assets include animals such as deer, bear, moose, timber wolf and trout, as well as a variety of trees—ash, maple, birch cherry and pine. Several old roads, which lumberjacks probably used, traverse the forest from the shore of Lake Superior. Known as the Sawbill, Arrowhead, Caribou and Gunflint Trails, these roads may be used today. The visitor can also watch for a few of the hundreds of Chippewa pictographs (ancient or prehistoric drawings or paintings on rock walls) scattered throughout the forest.

The Superior National Forest includes the Boundary Waters Canoe Area, set aside as a wilderness preservation area by the Wilderness Act of 1964. This area in northern Minnesota borders the Canadian Quetico Provincial Park (see entry 28).

The Boundary Waters Canoe Area, comprising one-third of the Superior National Forest, is the largest wilderness area in the United States so richly endowed with lakes and streams. Voyageurs National Park adjoins the Superior National Forest at its western-most point. Canoeing enthusiasts will find that the waters of the Quetico, Superior National Forest and Voyageurs National Park offer a challenging opportunity to ply the same water routes as the voyageurs.

Just what impact the discovery and exploitation of valuable copper-nickel deposits in the Superior National Forest will have upon the forest and boundary waters canoe areas remains to be seen.

"Picture Rock, Crooked Lake," painted by Francis L. Jacques, shows a well-traveled Voyageurs National Park waterway.

13. VOYAGEURS NATIONAL PARK

[Accessible from Hy 61 via Hy 1 and Hy 53 or from Duluth via Hy 53 to International Falls, (H-C-F-B)]

Covering an area of more than 219,000 acres of glaciated lake, stream and forest country, Voyageurs National Park offers unusual opportunities to study geological history. This lake-studded park lies in the midst of the waterways traversed by the voyageurs.

Logged in the 1880s, the parklands have a good wood cover of aspen, birch, balsam, white spruce, maple, black spruce, white cedar, ash and tamarack. The clear lakes and streams offer unusually fine opportunities for canoeing. Here moose, whitetailed deer and black bear may be seen, as well as sizeable numbers of beaver, mink, otter, bobcats and rabbits. Major sport fish include the walleye, northern pike and smallmouth bass. The principal birds inhabiting the park are grouse, mallards, black ducks, mergansers and loons. Park headquarters is located at International Falls, Minnesota.

14. SCHROEDER
[Hy 61]

For many years, logs which were harvested for the John Schroeder Lumber Company were rafted across Lake Superior to docks at Superior or Ashland from this point. However, this practice was discontinued in more recent times because rail transportation seemed faster than the one mile-per-hour speed attained by the log rafts.

A granite cross here marks the spot where Father Frederic Baraga (see "The Pioneer Missionaries," p. 106) reached shore after a stormy lake crossing in 1846. In gratitude for his safety, Chippewa Indians erected a bark cross on the shore (see L'Anse, entry 71).

15. TEMPERANCE RIVER STATE PARK
[Hy 61, (P-H-C-F)]

This river received its name because it was believed to be the only river running into Lake Superior that did not have a bar at its mouth. There are nature trails in the park and a spectacular rocky gorge where the river drops in a series of cascades a distance of 162 feet in a half mile.

16. RAY BERGLUND STATE MEMORIAL
[Hy 61, (H-C)]

The Berglund family donated this land to the state in memory of this St. Paul lumberman who loved the area.

17. CASCADE RIVER STATE PARK
[Hy 61, (P-H-C-F)]

The lovely waterfalls near the mouth of the Cascade River prompted the name of the river and the state

Cascade River.

The harbor at Grand Marais.

park as well. The park contains four miles of hiking trails and 12 miles of scenic shoreline.

18. GRAND MARAIS
[Hy 61]

The excellent natural harbor at Grand Marais was recognized early in its history. Federal surveyors visiting the area found a trading post here in 1859. The U.S. Coast Guard station welcomes visitors.

19. KONDONCE STATE PARK
[Hy 61, (P-H-F)]

Kondonce Creek is a favorite stream for trout fishermen.

20. JUDGE C. R. MAGNEY STATE PARK
[Hy 61, (P-H-C-F-S)]

While serving as mayor of Duluth, Judge C. R. Magney assisted in the establishment of 11 state parks along the north shore of Lake Superior. Although all the parks are famed for their natural beauty, the carved lava rock formations are of particular interest here. Water from the Brule River (there are Brule Rivers in both Minnesota and Wisconsin, as well as a third Brule River which forms part of the Wisconsin-Michigan border) plunges 70 feet down to a huge pothole worn into the rock and then disappears; for this reason it is known as Devil's Kettle.

21. GRAND PORTAGE INDIAN RESERVATION

This Chippewa reservation, one of six organized to form the Minnesota Chippewa Tribe under the 1934 Indian Reorganization Act, has a population of 189 Indians living on or near the reservation. The reservation area covers 44,752 acres. The tribe owns 37,390 acres of land and the government owns 79 acres. The remaining 7,283 acres are deeded to individual Indians, with restrictions placed upon the land's transfer.

Timber and gravel are the only natural resources on reservation lands. The tribe operates the Grand Portage Marina, a guide service and a 100-room resort hotel. Guests can hunt and fish on the reservation. The tribe also operates a picnic and trailer park about 38 miles north of Grand Marais. Grand Portage Reservation Indians hold Summer Rendezvous Days annually to commemorate the great days of the fur trade.

Also on the reservation stands OUR LADY OF THE ROSARY CATHOLIC CHURCH*, part of the oldest Roman Catholic parish in Minnesota, for which Father Baraga secured a resident priest. The present church, built of tamarack logs covered with siding, replaced the original in 1865. The interior was renovated in 1954 by adding an oak floor and electricity. The congregation numbers nearly 100, mostly from the reservation. During the summer, a student from St. John's Abbey, located 290 miles away at Collegeville, Minnesota, holds mass daily, but during the winter a priest serves the church only on Sundays when weather permits.

Another structure worth seeing is the GRAND PORTAGE ELEMENTARY SCHOOL — one of less than a dozen log schools still in use in the United States. It stands on a hill on the reservation and commands a beautiful view of Lake Superior. The classroom building was built in 1928 of western red cedar logs on a native stone foundation.

22. GRAND PORTAGE NATIONAL MONUMENT

[Hy 61]

The Grand Portage National Monument stands as a reminder of the eighteenth century French and British fur traders and voyageurs. Following the lure of the beaver, they plied the waters of the Great Lakes and the inland rivers and streams from Montreal to Fort Chipewyan on Lake Athabaska in the northwest wilderness, some 3,000 miles away. The Grand Portage, the "great carrying place," is a nine-mile trail which bypasses some 20 miles of waterfalls and rapids near the mouth of the Pigeon River on Lake Superior.

The portage was first used and named by French fur traders and explorers in the seventeenth century, and first mentioned in writing by Jean Pachot in 1722. Sieur de la Vérendrye used the portage in 1732 and thereafter the French traders used it in preference to the Kaministikwia route into the wilderness of the Canadian northwest (see Fort William, entry 26). Visitors may hike the portage trail today.

British traders first used the Grand Portage route in 1762, one year before the French withdrew from

"Canoes in a Fog," painted by Frances Hopkins, an Englishwoman who married a Hudson's Bay Company official.

Canada. For the next four decades the Montreal traders used the route, establishing posts on Grand Portage Bay and at the trail's end on the Pigeon River. Grand Portage became a rendezvous point for Montreal fur traders about 1767. In 1779 the Montreal-based North West Company made the site on the south bank of the Pigeon River its inland headquarters.

During the North West Company's use of the Grand Portage-Pigeon River route, its headquarters served as an exchange point for trade goods from Montreal and furs from the northwest wilderness.

An annual exchange of goods took place in mid-July. Along with the serious business went feasting, fighting and the merriment of the rendezvous. The return trips east and west began August 1. Fortunes were made in the Grand Portage fur trade and the North West Company prospered.

Although the portage was claimed as American territory under the Treaty of Paris in 1783, the North West Company continued to use the location until 1803. Then, fearing American taxation, the company moved its headquarters to Fort William and utilized the Kaministikwia route.

The Webster-Ashburton Treaty in 1842 settled many boundary disputes between the United States and British Canada, including the ambiguously described area lying between Lake Superior and the Lake of the Woods. While the Pigeon River became part of that international boundary, the terms of the 1842 treaty specified that the portage be free and open for use by both Americans and Canadians. The decision came late; the buildings of the North West Company had decayed and the portage trade had greatly dwindled.

At Grand Portage National Monument visitors can see the restored stockade, a fur press, canoe warehouse, kitchen, the dock and the Great Hall, where the partners of the North West Company — the respected aristocrats of the business — met to do company business, to feast and to dance. Dedicated as a national monument in 1960, Grand Portage is operated by the National Park Service.

(Numbered entries continued on p. 40)

Great Hall at Grand Portage.

THE FUR TRADE, 1763-1840

Prize of the fur trade.

After French political control of the Lake Superior region ceased in 1763, the French contribution to the fur trade remained significant. At first the British, and later the Americans, reaped the benefits of the earlier French regime. The French had opened the fur trade routes and become experts at trading with the Indians. Because of this experience, French business partners were deliberately sought by British and American fur traders. Also vital to the trade were the skilled French canoemen, or voyageurs, many of whom came from communities along the lower St. Lawrence River.

From the close of the French and Indian War until 1817, the British dominated the fur trade of Lake Superior, even though the southern lakeshore became American territory in 1783. This period of British domination took shape in the early 1760s as French soldiers evacuated their posts on the upper Great Lakes. At first British policy was to restrict the fur trade to large posts. One British partnership formed by Alexander Henry and John Baptiste Cadotte, an experienced French trader, received exclusive rights to the fur trade on Lake Superior in 1765. The partnership operated out of Mackinac, the designated center for the Lake Superior trade.

But in 1767 the British changed their policy and threw the trade open to licensed traders. This brought a rush of small companies into the area and spawned a period of savage competition. The number of trading partnerships, operating out of Mackinac, grew from four in 1770 to seven in 1775. At Grand Portage in 1775, Alexander Henry "found the traders in a state of extreme reciprocal hostility, each pursuing his interests in such a manner as might most injure his neighbor. The consequences were very hurtful to the morals of the Indians."

Out of this ruinous competition grew the North West Company, established in 1779. A large, loosely organized company, headquartered in Montreal, it had many partners—most of them Scotsmen and British colonials. Until 1803, the company's major western post was at Grand Portage and, thereafter, at Fort William. The North West Company also established secondary posts at many sites around Lake Superior on both the U.S. and Canadian sides. This vast operation involved more than a thousand traders and voyageurs and many guides, interpreters and clerks as well. The company enjoyed its greatest prosperity between 1780 and 1820. A visit to the Grand Portage Monument in Minnesota or Fort William at Thunder Bay, Ontario, will give the visitor an excellent idea of the operations of the North West Company during its heyday (see entries 22 and 26).

The vigorous and aggressive North West Company quickly found itself in competition with the Hudson's Bay Company—the great royal fur trading monopoly that governed all the territory drained by streams emptying into Hudson Bay. A unified and tightly-organized business, the Hudson's Bay Company had already enjoyed a century of experience in the fur trade by 1780. It moved quickly to try to establish itself in the Lake Superior region. In the 1790s, it built posts in the Rainy Lake area northwest of Fort William.

The strong conflict and bitter rivalry between the two companies was resolved when the British government forced them to merge in 1821. Thereafter, the Hudson's Bay Company handled all Canadian fur trade on Lake Superior and operated on American shores as well under agreements with the American Fur Company. For a variety of reasons, the Hudson's Bay Company eventually focused its activity in the more profitable fur trading regions of Western Canada and deemphasized Lake Superior. The value of Lake Superior area furs declined and Fort William fell into decay.

The major competitor of the North West and Hudson's Bay companies was the American Fur Company with posts serving the Lake Superior trade at Mackinac, Sault Ste. Marie and Fond du Lac (now Duluth). John Jacob Astor headed the company from its founding in 1808 until 1834. Following the War of 1812, Astor wanted to control the fur trade of the Great Lakes, a goal which had eluded him because of British competition. He had also failed in competition with the British in the Pacific Northwest's Columbia River Valley, and had been forced to sell his fur trading post, Astoria, at the mouth of the Columbia River to the North West Company in 1813. In 1817 Astor entered the Great Lakes fur trade with a score to settle. He had the dubious advantage of a federal law, enacted in 1816, that excluded foreigners from the American trade. The British had to remain north of the border and yet Astor's success depended on non-Americans experienced in the fur trade. So repeatedly he took advantage of a clause in the law which permitted the licensing of foreigners for American trade on an annual basis.

At the time of Astor's entrance into the Great Lakes fur trade, its heyday had already passed. By 1816 there were great pressures to remove the Indians and to open American lands to farmer-settlers. Also, the beaver population was dwindling. As a result, the American Fur Company's activity in the Lake Superior fur trade was short-lived. The

Entrance gate, Grand Portage.

Company did well in the 1820s and in 1833 Astor decided to retire. Ramsay Crooks assumed leadership of a new American Fur Company in 1834, but the company failed in 1842. Its liquidation, like the retrenchment of the Hudson's Bay Company in the Superior area, signalled a marked decline in the importance of the fur trade in the region. By then, other great natural resources of the Lake Superior shores—timber, copper and iron—stood on the brink of exploitation. Mining, in particular, added a new vitality to the region even as the revelry of the rendevouz and the songs of the voyageurs faded away.

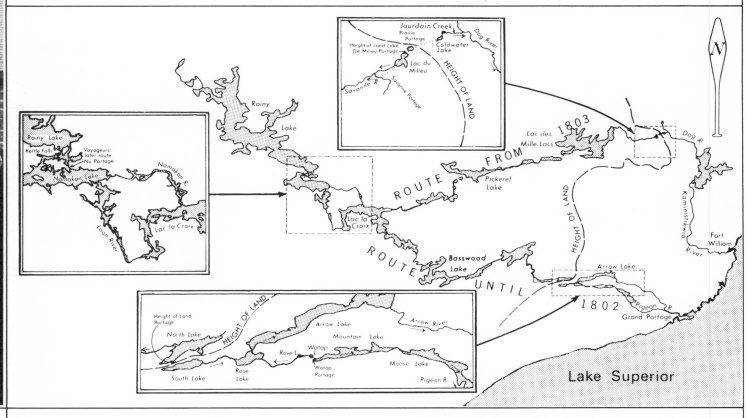

Fur trade routes west from Grand Portage and Fort William.

Voyageurs National Park.

23. ISLE ROYALE NATIONAL PARK

(P-H-C-F-B)

The territory covered by Isle Royale includes a large island, 45 by 9 miles in area, as well as five chains of smaller islands. Claimed by French explorers and named by them in honor of King Louis XIV, Isle Royale later became British territory and, by the Treaty of 1783, part of the United States. A number of writers have suggested that Benjamin Franklin, knowing of the rich copper deposits on Isle Royale, managed to include it in American territory at the Paris peace negotiations in 1783, but this idea has been cast aside. The more accepted explanation is that it became an American possession because the natural water dividing line between the U.S. and Canada ran north of Isle Royale. When Michigan became a state in 1837, Isle Royale was included in its territory. The island became a national park in 1931.

Copper mines on Isle Royale, which had been worked by the Indians, were discovered by prospectors who continued to extract copper between 1845 and 1899. The most prominent of the mine sites, Minong Mine*, was worked in the 1870s and may still be seen at McCargoe Cove on the north shore of the island. Visitors may also come across former mine sites elsewhere on the island. A chunk of copper from Isle Royale weighing 5,720 pounds was displayed at the Centennial Exposition in Philadelphia in 1876 and aroused much interest.

There is a variety of flora and fauna on the island, the most interesting of which are the moose and grey timber wolf populations. Six hundred moose are believed to have come across the ice from Canada at some time in the past. Because hunters may not shoot moose on Isle Royale, the animals at one time threatened to overpopulate the island. However, grey timber wolves restored a natural population balance following their appearance there in 1950. Although this species has been in danger of becoming extinct on the island, the number of wolves has now increased to about 20.

Transportation to Isle Royale is by boat or seaplane. Boat connections originate from Houghton and Copper Harbor, Michigan and Grand Portage, Minnesota. Because of weather conditions, the island is abandoned between October and February. During the summer season, camp sites and two lodges offer facilities for overnight guests. Interpretive programs include campfire talks by naturalists, trailside exhibits and self-guiding nature trails. Over 80 miles of hiking trails lead to inland lakes, historic mine sites, geological formations or fire lookout towers. The longest trail, Greenstone Ridge, stretches over 36 miles. Twenty-five miles of trout streams tantalize the fisherman.

Rock of Ages Lighthouse*, on the southwestern tip of the island, is considered to be one of the most spectacular lighthouses on Lake Superior. It stands 117 feet high on a reef as an aid to passing ships.

Isle Royale's Rock of Ages Lighthouse.

24. PIGEON FALLS

[Hy 61]

The United States—Canada customs reception center is here. Persons crossing the international border must stop and check in with customs and immigration authorities at this point.

Ontario, Canada

Entries 25-45

A favorite summer campsite, Middle Falls Provincial Park.

25. MIDDLE FALLS PROVINCIAL PARK

[Hy 61, (P-H-C-F-B-S)]

This ten-acre recreation park on the Ontario-Minnesota border is located below the middle of three waterfalls on the lower 21 miles of the Pigeon River. A seven-mile hiking trail along the river passes beautiful cascades and an old log sluiceway three miles downstream. There is also a fine view of the higher falls on the river.

26. THUNDER BAY

[Hy 61]

The origins of the city of Thunder Bay date from the early nineteenth century when the North West Company moved its inland headquarters from Grand Portage (see entry 22) to a location on the north bank of the Kaministikwia River near its mouth on Thunder Bay.

Fort William, the new inland headquarters of the company, became the site of the annual rendezvous, where furs collected during the winter months and trade goods from Montreal changed hands, and where the wintering partners and the Montreal partners conducted the business of the company and made plans for the coming year. The fur trade gave commercial vitality to the wilderness environment at Fort William until 1821 when the North West Company amalgamated with the Hudson's Bay Company.

From that time until the mid-1800s, Fort William underwent a steady decline in importance in the fur trade, largely because profits from furs in the Thunder Bay district gradually declined. The Hudson's Bay Company chose to make Hudson Bay the chief outlet for furs and to de-emphasize the Lake Superior region in preference to others.

Hopes for renewal of prosperity rose at Fort William in the mid-1840s when the Lake Superior region became a focus for potential mining development. The townsite at Fort William was again surveyed. Its townspeople numbered only a few: some settlers and a number of Chippewa Indians, all associated in one way or another with the fur trade or with providing transportation westward for travelers over the water routes so familiar to the voyageurs.

While the early hopes for mining faded in 1850, another new development soon promised a commercial revolution. In 1855 the opening of the canal at Sault Ste. Marie made Lake Superior far more accessible to the developing commercial areas of Canada and the United States to the east and south.

During the 1860s the Canadian government sought a route which would tie the wilderness of Lake Superior and territories lying to the west with eastern Canada. The town of Prince Arthur's Landing thus came into being. Located on Thunder Bay a few miles inland from Fort William, Prince Arthur's Landing was designed initially to be the terminus of a road running inland from Thunder Bay to Dog Lake.

The Louis Riel rebellion at Red River provided the stimulus for translating talk about better transportation into action. The Americans refused to let Canadians use the Sault canal for troop movements. The subsequent difficulties of traveling overland from Fort William led ultimately to the construction of the Canadian Pacific Railroad skirting the northern edge of Lake Superior. The line was completed between Thunder Bay and Winnepeg in 1882.

Again, the Thunder Bay area found itself cast in the role of a transshipment point, this time for wheat shipped east from the developing prairie provinces and for westward-bound cargoes and passengers,

The steamboat ALGOMA, transporting Canadian troops past Thunder Cape in 1870.

including immigrant settlers moving through Fort William and Prince Arthur's Landing.

Prince Arthur's Landing soon became Port Arthur, a more convenient name for railroad passenger tickets and signs. It was equipped with docks and storage facilities and the Canadian Pacific arranged for a plentiful supply of lake boats. The coming of the railroad fanned the flames of jealousy between the fort and the port as each sought to secure the location of railroad facilities. For a time the port seemed to be winning, but in 1891 Fort William secured the terminal buildings and workshops.

Meanwhile, the Thunder Bay area had developed economically, based on its own natural resources. From the 1870s until 1890 it was the center of a silver mining craze. As mining declined, agricultural development made modest beginnings. In the 1890s a survey of the vast timber resources in the area began, resources hitherto regarded as unworthy of development. Lumbering grew as silver mining declined.

Port Arthur incorporated as a town in 1884 and Fort William incorporated in 1892. Burying the old animosities of bustling port and prestigious fort, Port Arthur and Fort William merged in 1970. The citizens chose by ballot the name Thunder Bay in preference to Lakehead or The Lakehead.

Today, Thunder Bay prospers as a busy industrial port city, the sixth largest in Ontario. It boasts the largest working grain elevator in the world. Saskatchewan Pool 7, and a number of smaller elevators. (Guided tours may be arranged with the Saskatchewan Pool elevators.) Facilities today are a far cry from those in existence when the first wheat from Manitoba arrived in 1883. Ore docks built by the Canadian Pacific Railroad accommodate iron ore from the Steep Rock Lake mines north of Atikokan, which were opened for mining during World War II. The lumbering industry has gone through a transformation from its earliest days, and Thunder Bay has become a center for Canadian paper and pulp production.

Thunder Bay, Ontario.

THUNDER BAY SITES OF INTEREST

Fort William Historical Park, on Broadway Avenue west of Hy 61. When the North West Company decided to move its inland headquarters from Grand Portage (see entry 22), the north bank, near the mouth of the Kaministikwia River, offered real advantages as a new site. Here Fort William became established. This same area had earlier appealed to Daniel Greysolon, Sieur du Lhut, and Zacharie Robutel de la Noue as a strategically suitable trading and exploring base. They used the Kaministikwia River for access to the wilderness of the North-west.

Between 1803 and 1821 Fort William served as a busy center for the fur trade. The company built an elaborate stockaded headquarters consisting of some 40 buildings. After 1821, when the North West Company amalgamated with the Hudson's Bay Company, Fort William gradually fell into ruin from neglect and disuse.

One traveler reported in 1843: "Ranges of sheds and stores are empty and the old mess house, 60 feet long, in which so many hardy traders used to tell of their exploits, is now a shed of canoes, half a ruin." Remains of the fort disappeared completely between 1883 and 1902, making way for the facilities of the Canadian Pacific Railway.

A few miles from the original site of Fort William, the Province of Ontario has embarked upon one of the largest restoration projects in North America.

Dressed as a chief trader, a guide welcomes visitors to Fort William.

The restoration team used the fort's original plans in an attempt to be as accurate as possible in their reconstruction. This "living history" site consists of some 40 structures, including a stockaded working complex, adjacent farm buildings and wharf.

A large staff recreates the lifestyles of the eighteenth century: clerks, bakers, tailors, company partners, gunsmiths, blacksmiths, coopers and carpenters may be seen at work, bringing the fort to life for visitors.

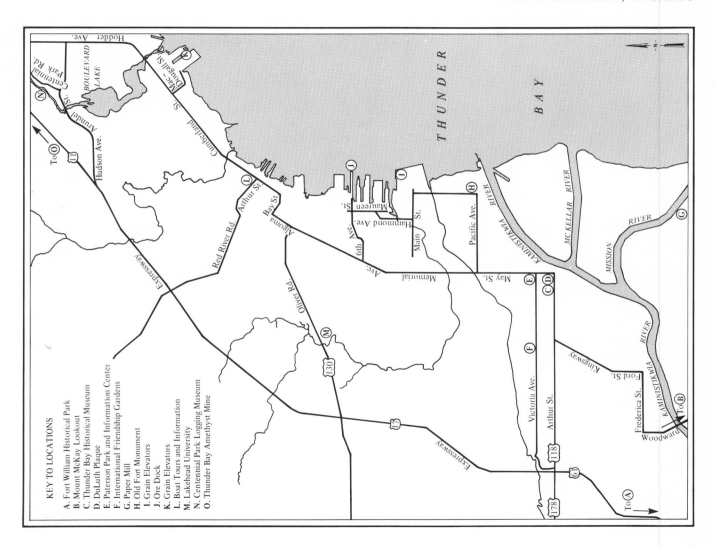

KEY TO LOCATIONS

A. Fort William Historical Park
B. Mount McKay Lookout
C. Thunder Bay Historical Museum
D. DuLuth Plaque
E. Paterson Park and Information Center
F. International Friendship Gardens
G. Paper Mill
H. Old Fort Monument
I. Grain Elevators
J. Ore Dock
K. Grain Elevators
L. Boat Tours and Information
M. Lakehead University
N. Centennial Park Logging Museum
O. Thunder Bay Amethyst Mine

Frederic Remington's "Voyageurs in Camp for the Night," first published in *Harper's New Monthly Magazine* in 1892.

The visitor can also see the business operations of the North West Company, details of its trade, displays of trade goods and furs, demonstrations of the work of the voyageurs, plus the drama of their rendezvous, and even the actual construction of Montreal canoes. Open daily from mid-June to mid-September, ($). (Although an unusual, dev-astating flood covered the site in the summer of 1977, Fort William has reopened almost all of its historic buildings to the public).

Mount McKay, 1,600 feet above sea level, is reached by Hy 61B through the Chippewa Indian Reservation. A Memorial Chapel in memory of Indians killed during World War II stands on a ridge partway up the mountain. The Mission Band of Indians also operates a camping area.

Thunder Bay Historical Museum, 219 May Street South, displays worthwhile collections of prehistoric Indian and Silver Islet mining materials.

DuLhut Plaque, in front of City Hall, Thunder Bay. This plaque reminds visitors that DuLhut, the famous French explorer whose name is most often associated with Duluth, Minnesota, built the first post at the mouth of the Kaministikwia River in 1679.

Paterson Park. A piper from one of the bagpipe bands of Thunder Bay entertains daily, at noon in summer.

International Friendship Gardens, 1800-2000 Victoria Avenue. The varied ethnic groups which make the Thunder Bay area their home constructed these gardens as a centennial gift to Canada. The city of Thunder Bay donated land on Reflection Lake in 1966 and the Polish community completed the first garden in 1971. By 1976, ten ethnic groups had completed gardens, each with ethnically characteristic plantings and statuary. Other ethnic groups may add to the gardens in the future.

Great Hall, Fort William.

Both Quetico Provincial Park and Boundary Waters Canoe Area are a canoeist's dream.

Thunder Bay Harbor. Boat tours of Thunder Bay leave from the foot of Hy 102.

Centennial Park Logging Museum, Current River Road. This 1910 lumber camp reconstruction opens May-September. ($)

Thunder Bay Amethyst Mine, six miles from Hy 17 on East Loon Road. While land was being cleared for a fire tower on Elbow Lake about 35 miles east of Thunder Bay, a bulldozer uncovered a vein of purple amethyst. The area invites rock collectors who may search for specimens on their own. A rock shop is available for those who prefer to buy rock specimens. Even the unsuccessful "rock hound" will find the jagged amethyst vein cut into solid red granite and the view of Elbow Lake well worth seeing.

27. KAKABEKA FALLS PROVINCIAL PARK

[18 miles west of Thunder Bay (P-H-C-F-S)]

Dropping 128 feet, the Kakabeka Falls plunge into the Kaministikwia River below. Sometimes called the "Niagara of the North," the falls create a greenish mist that floats up about them. Legends about Green Mantle, a Chippewa Indian maiden, are associated with the mist.

28. QUETICO PROVINCIAL PARK

[Hy 11, west from Thunder Bay (P-H-C-F-B-S)]

Indians, explorers, fur traders, immigrants and soldiers crossed this wilderness area of lakes, rivers and forests--a major section of the route west. Simon Dawson surveyed a road and water route in 1857 to carry settlers between Prince Arthur's Landing and Fort Garry in Manitoba. He used the route of the fur traders which passed through the center of what is now Quetico Provincial Park, but the necessary construction work on the dams, locks and roads was not completed for settlers until 1870.

Named as a provincial park in 1913, the Quetico recently became classified as a primitive park, emphasizing its wilderness qualities. In particular, it attracts canoe enthusiasts and fishermen. Throughout the area the visitor can see rugged glacial formations, dashing rivers and streams, the flora and fauna of a hardwood forest and Indian pictographs at 28 different locations. Created by ancestors of the Cree and Chippewa people, these pictographs depict moose, heron, deer, caribou, Indian warriors, homes and canoes. A museum at the Dawson Trail campgrounds at French Lake contains exhibits which explain the area's history.

From Thunder Bay to Sault Ste. Marie: The Natural Setting. At Thunder Bay the traveler of the Lake Superior circuit visits the last major historic site before arriving in the Sault Ste. Marie area. From Thunder Bay to the Sault lies a largely wild area of great natural beauty. Sparsely populated with only an occasional pulp mill, mining enterprise or hydroelectric plant, the northern and eastern edges of Lake Superior offer many delights to those who enjoy the northwoods scenery. Cliffs, ravines, waterfalls, hills, mountains, beaches, lakes, islands, and bays can be seen here. This area is Lake Superior woodlands and waters at their best.

Although more than 125 years have passed since Louis Agassiz made a canoeing expedition to study the natural history of the northern shore of Lake Superior, many comments of the expedition's chronicler still hold true. The party worked its way westward and northward from Sault Ste. Marie, noting that at Goulais Bay the shoreline took on a "mountainous" character:

"So different was the scene from anything on the Lower Lakes that, although I knew in general that the shore of Lake Superior was much bolder and more rocky than that of the others, yet it took me by surprise, and I was disposed to think this part of it an exception, until assured, by one who had been here before, that the grandeur of the scenery constantly increased to the northward.... [From the northern extremity of Batchawana Bay onward, the shoreline,] down to the very beach, was covered with trees. Indeed, I may say once and for all, that with the exception of some ancient terraces of fine sand and gravel to be described hereafter, and a few summits of bare rock, the entire shore of Lake Superior [to Fort William], is continuously covered with forest. The trees continued the same, except that the white pines and maples disappeared. The number of species is small; black and white spruce, balsam fir, canoe birch, and aspen, with arbor vitae in the moist places, and here and there a few larches and red pines, with an occasional yellow birch; the spruces prevailing on the high land, and the birch and aspen near the water....The trees are not large, usually not exceeding thirty or forty feet in height. Yet the whole effect is rich and picturesque. Here, as in all the features of the lake, the impression is a grand uniformity, never monotonous, but expressive of its unique character."

"Grand" and "unique" are still the words to describe Superior's northern shore. A series of eleven provincial parks lying on or near the main route from Thunder Bay to Sault Ste. Marie preserve much of this grandeur.

The Louis Agassiz expedition on Lake Superior as depicted in Agassiz's book, *Lake Superior,* published in 1850.

29. SIBLEY PENINSULA

[Hy 587, 24 miles east of Thunder Bay]

SILVER ISLET AND SIBLEY PROVINCIAL PARK (P-H-C-F-B-S)

The 25-mile long peninsula was named for Alexander Hamilton Sibley, president of the Silver Islet Mining Company. Although his permanent home was in Detroit, Sibley maintained a 21-room mansion at the southeastern tip of the peninsula that looked out across Lake Superior to tiny Silver Islet.

Originally the property of the Montreal Mining Company, Silver Islet was purchased by an American syndicate and in 1869 mining operations began. The mine produced almost a million dollars worth of ore in 1870 and 1871 and a total of three million dollars worth during its years of operation from 1869-1884. Mining operations--which had always been conducted in competition with the waters of Lake Superior--ceased in the winter of 1884 when a severe storm wrecked equipment and flooded the mine.

The only remaining buildings from these mining operations are miners' houses on the mainland, now used as summer cottages at the village of Silver Islet. Following the departure of the miners, lumbering operations began, but these ended in the 1930s.

In 1944 the peninsula became a provincial park. Today, the park covers 94 square miles. Park

"Sea Lion" rock formation near Silver Islet.

Sleeping Giant as viewed from Sibley Provincial Park.

visitors are offered a wide variety of activities and may choose between four marked nature trails and nine blazed hiking trails, as well as two automobile drives leading to lookouts across Thunder Bay and from the bluffs at Pass Lake.

An inland lake in the park, Lake Marie Louise, offers a fine swimming beach as well as many campsites. Other primitive campsites are scattered throughout the park. Moose, deer, bear and many other animals inhabit the parklands. Birds abound--200 species of them--and the visitor can enjoy observing plant species that usually grow much farther north. Park naturalists hold interpretive programs in the park amphitheater during summer.

The best known rock formation on the peninsula is a series of sedimentary rock mesas known as the Sleeping Giant, a 20-mile long mountainous cape. From the top of the Sleeping Giant, visitors can look out across miles of Lake Superior to Isle Royale to the south, or northward over the park's many lakes and green forests.

The Sleeping Giant is named for Nanabazhoo, an important legendary figure to the Chippewa Indians who once lived on the peninsula. One legend says that Nanabazhoo, a protector of the Chippewa, was turned to stone by the Great Spirit when white men were told of the presence of silver there. Another version relates that Nanabazhoo killed his

Encrusted saxifrage, an Arctic plant found in Ouimet Canyon.

wife in a fit of temper and ran in terror from his wigwam into the night. He kept seeing visions of his murdered wife and in fright and remorse he staggered and fell back into the lake waters. The Great Spirit took pity on him and turned him into everlasting stone.

30.   OUIMET CANYON PROVINCIAL PARK

[Hy 17, (P-F)]

Of the eight nature reserve parks in the province of Ontario, only Ouimet Canyon is open to the public. There are no facilities for camping, but park visitors may climb a trail to a lookout point high above the canyon for an extraordinary view into its 350-foot depths, where tons of rock have fallen to the valley floor. The 500-foot wide, tree-lined canyon is a two-mile long cleft in volcanic rock created by wind, water and ice. Because of the low temperatures in the canyon, some species of Arctic plants have been found here.

31.   NIPIGON AND RED ROCK

[Hy 11]

The Nipigon-Red Rock area provides unusually fine scenic viewing for the traveler. There are islands, mountain masses of the Precambrian shield, the waters of Nipigon Bay and Red Rock Cuesta lying south of Nipigon. The latter is a 700-foot high, two-mile long cliff with a granite base and horizontal layers of bright red limestone. Nipigon, the site of a very old French post, later became a minor post of the Hudson's Bay Company. Both Catholics and

Protestants established missions near here. Although the fur trading posts have long since vanished, a museum at Nipigon contains interesting displays on the logging era.

A side trip off the main highway along Hy 585 is worthwhile for its view of the very unusual bright red limestone cliffs at Red Rock. The road follows the Nipigon River to Pine Portage. The falls and rapids of the Nipigon, although now harnessed for hydroelectric power, still display much of the beauty noted by nineteenth century travelers.

32. ROSSPORT CAMPGROUND PROVINCIAL PARK

[Hy 17, (P-C-B-S)]

This campground is situated right on Lake Superior. At the mouth of Nipigon Bay members of the Agassiz Expedition found the St. Ignace Island area extraordinarily beautiful in 1848. At St. Ignace, "high in front, black to the top with spruce forests," the chronicler reported, they found an abandoned mining location. Landing their canoes, they ascended a peak 1,300 feet high and christened it Mount Cambridge, finding the summit "steep and rocky, the rocks polished and scratched at the top."

33. RAINBOW FALLS PROVINCIAL PARK

[Hy 17, eight miles west of Schreiber,(P-H-C-F-B-S)]

This park provides camping and picnicking facilities on White Sand Lake. There are two self-guiding nature trails for hikers as well as trout fishing in the Selim River. A trail to Rainbow Falls continues on to a lookout, where there is a spectacular view of the hills, forest, river and Lake Superior islands. Moose and other wildlife inhabit the park.

34. TERRACE BAY

[Hy 17]

When the Swiss-born naturalist, Louis Agassiz, led his expedition to Lake Superior in 1848, they camped in the Terrace Bay area in July. Here they found a lush growth of bearberry on the sandy beach "with balsam firs and larches judiciously disposed at intervals." Having seen the effects of glaciers in his native Switzerland, Agassiz concluded that the glacier had caused the terraces he found here. He described them as three main terraces and several subordinate ones, reaching a maximum height of 331 feet above the level of the lake. Geologists say that four huge ice sheets which covered the area during the Ice Age left behind the sand and gravel terraces from which the town takes its name.

From Centennial Park in the center of town the visitor can view the multicolored escarpments containing amethysts, tyrolite, quartz and opalite between the terraces.

In 1949 a community was carved out of the wilderness here for employees of a bleached sulphate pulp mill operated by Kimberly-Clark of Canada, Ltd. Kimberly-Clark conducts daily tours.

This lithograph from Agassiz's *Lake Superior,* published in 1850, shows the lake terraces left by the glaciers.

35. NEYS PROVINCIAL PARK

[15 miles west of Marathon, Hy 17, (P-C-F-B-S)]

This Natural Environment Park† has especially fine scenic and wildlife features. There are woodland caribou, now scarce along the shore of Lake Superior, red fox and rainbow trout. One self-guided nature trail leads to a high hill with a view and another leads to a beaver dam. Neys Provincial Park includes the site of a World War II prisoner of war camp.

†Canadian Natural Environment Provincial Parks contain outstanding aesthetic, natural and historical features for recreation and education. These parks provide facilities for camping, picnicking, hiking and nature interpretation [Canadian government definition.]

36. MARATHON

[Hy 17]

The town of Peninsula Harbor sprang to life as a supply depot in the mid-1880s with the construction of the Canadian Pacific Railroad. But thereafter it languished. In 1945 a new community was constructed on this site and renamed Marathon. Marathon soon filled with employees of the bleached sulphate pulp mill and chemical plant operated by American Can of Canada, Ltd. The mill welcomes visitors.

37. PUKASKWA NATIONAL PARK

[Access will be from Hy 17 by a connecting road leading to a point near the mouth of the White River]

This national park, now under development, is one of 22 national parks in Canada dedicated to the Canadian people for the preservation of wildlife and historic sites. Pukaskwa National Park contains 725 square miles of land along the rugged Lake Superior shoreline. It includes bays, beaches, waterfalls, wild rivers, creeks and islands. Planned as a

White-tailed deer.

wilderness area, it will contain an abundance of wild flora and fauna and will offer camping, hiking, canoeing and nature study.

38. WHITE LAKE PROVINCIAL PARK

[2-1/2 miles south of Hy 17, (P-H-C-F-B-S)]

This park lies in unusually beautiful lake country and provides many opportunities for outdoor activities. White Lake was the site of an ancient Chippewa settlement and today the Mobert Indian Reserve shares White Lake with the provincial park. Campers may visit the Hudson's Bay Post across the lake.

39. OBATANGA PROVINCIAL PARK

[Hy 17, 32 miles north of Wawa, (P-H-C-F-B-S)]

A northern forest of jack pine surrounds this Natural Environment Park. The visitor can enjoy the usual park activities, as well as the nature hikes, films and other programs which introduce waterfowl and wildlife, ponds and a maze of lakes found in this unusually beautiful provincial park.

40. MICHIPICOTEN RIVER

[Hy 17]

The Indian name, Michipicoten, has sometimes been said to refer to the great bluffs that rise high above Lake Superior and at other times has been thought to mean "Big Sandy Bay," a good description of the bay-harbor area. Michipicoten served as the principal post of the Hudson's Bay Company in the Lake

Canada goose.

Superior area after 1821. Travel from this point up the Michipicoten and Moose Rivers to James Bay took 16 days, a route used by the Hudson's Bay Company for exporting furs.

Today the town serves as a shipping point for ore from the Algoma Steel Corporation mines to the foundries at Sault Ste. Marie. The Algoma Ore Division of Algoma Steel at Wawa ranked as the second largest ore producer in the Lake Superior district of Ontario in 1973, producing over 2,000,000 long tons.

North shore of Lake Superior near Wawa.

41.   WAWA

[Hy 17]

The Indian name, Wawa, imitates the cry of the Canadian geese as they land on the water each year during their migratory flights.   The huge steel goose at the entrance to the town pays tribute to the flocks of geese which are seasonal visitors. The visitor can tour abandoned gold mines in summer.

42.   LAKE SUPERIOR PROVINCIAL PARK

[85 miles north of Sault Ste. Marie, Hy 17, (P-H-C-F-B-S)]

This 3,000-acre Natural Environment Park, established in 1944, contains self-guided nature trails and waterfalls.   Information centers for visitors mark the north and south entrances to the park. A variety of subarctic plants flourishes in the shadow of northward-facing cliffs at Old Woman Bay.

An access road and stairway enable visitors to view Indian pictographs at Agawa Bay — the most accessible location for viewing pictographs in the Lake Superior area.   Although it is not known exactly when these rock paintings were done, Henry Schoolcraft made a record of the site before 1850.   The rock paintings depict 50 Indians crossing Lake Superior and attacking another group of Indians.   The paintings were evidently done with red ochre, an iron oxide pigment, which the Indians applied with their fingers.   The artists were probably Chippewa or Cree Indians.

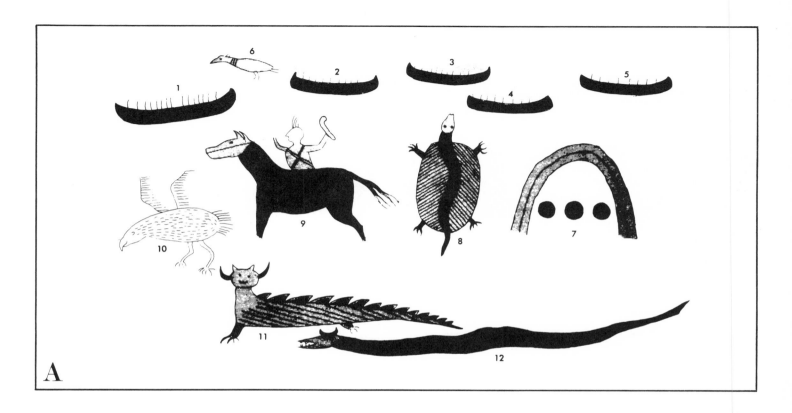

A

This sketch of the pictographs at the Agawa site in Lake Superior Provincial Park appeared in Henry Schoolcraft's *Indian Tribes of the United States,* (Volume I), published in 1851. Schoolcraft said that Chingwauk, a learned Indian who knew pictography, made these drawings on birch bark and gave them to him. While there are some differences between this Schoolcraft version and the original, they are minor. The drawings tell the story of a south shore Indian warrior, Myeengum, who organized a war party and crossed Lake Superior by canoe. The expedition included five canoes led by the kingfisher (figure 6). The crossing took three days, represented by the three suns under a sky and rainbow (7). The land tortoise may mean reaching land (8). Figure 9 show the Meda, holding a drum stick he used in magic rites, and riding a horse. The eagle (10) is the symbol of courage. Figures 11 and 12 record help received on the journey from a panther and a great serpent.

This pictograph also commemorates the Indian chief Myeengum's crossing of Lake Superior. According to Schoolcraft, this pictograph was located on the banks of the Carp River on Lake Superior's south shore. Anthropologists have searched for it in vain. Like that of pictograph A, this sketch was made on birch bark by Chingwauk and given to Schoolcraft. Figures 1, 2 and 3 represent the Chief Myeengum, his lodge and his totem. Figure 4 represents his name, "the wolf." The remaining eight figures are symbolic representations of various spirits or gods upon whom he relied. The panther, figure 5, has a human head with horns. The crosses on the body denote night, when the panther exercised its powers. Figure 6 is the panther without mane and crosses, and denotes the panther's power in the day. Figure 7 denotes reliance on the loon; 8, reliance on the black bear; and 9, reliance on the moose. The loon helped the warrior because its call forecast the weather. The bear stood for strength and sagacity; the moose for wariness. The great serpent, 10, symbolized swiftness and power over life, and the lizard, 11, had similar powers. The chief relied on all of these spirits or gods to make his successful crossing of Lake Superior.

43.   RANWICK URANIUM MINE

[Hy 17, 78 miles north of Sault Ste. Marie]

For years it had been suspected that there was pitch-blende in this region. Pitchblende is a brownish-black mineral that contains radium and is the chief natural source of uranium. In 1949, using his Geiger counter, Robert Campbell discovered pitchblende in the Theano Point area. Later discoverers found deposits in the neighborhood of Blind River.

Located deep underground, the Ranwick mine is the only uranium mine in Canada open to visitors. The visitor can also see demonstrations of the Geiger counter and may purchase radioactive ore samples. ($)

44.   PANCAKE BAY PROVINCIAL PARK

[Hy 17, 50 miles north of Sault Ste. Marie, (P-C-F-S)]

This park contains sandy beaches for swimming and rivers for trout fishing. Air temperatures are moderate, even during the hot summer months.

45.   BATCHAWANA BAY PROVINCIAL PARK

[Hy 17, (P-F-B-S)]

The 100-acre park offers fine sandy beaches and a good view of the lake. Here the visitor will find good boating, safe swimming and trout fishing. For day use only, no camping.

Lake Superior Provincial Park.

THE FRENCH IN THE GREAT LAKES COUNTRY

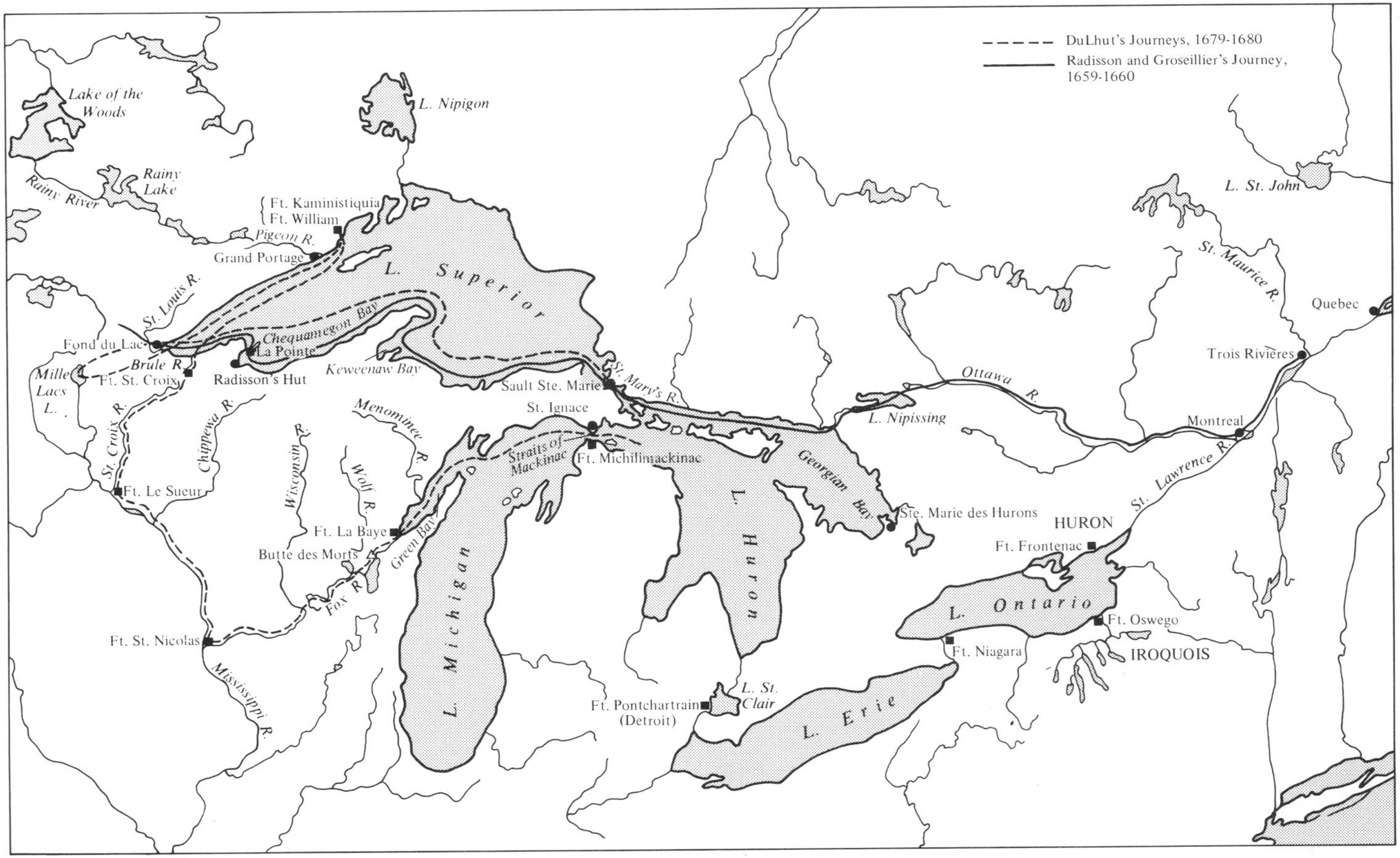

Lake of the Woods

L. Nipigon

Rainy Lake

Rainy River

L. St. John

- - - - - DuLhut's Journeys, 1679-1680
────── Radisson and Groseillier's Journey, 1659-1660

Ft. Kaministiquia
Ft. William
Pigeon R.
Grand Portage

St. Louis R.

St. Maurice R.

Quebec

L. Superior

Fond du Lac

Chequamegon Bay
La Pointe

Brule R.

Keweenaw Bay

Trois Rivières

Mille Lacs L.

Ft. St. Croix

Radisson's Hut

St. Mary's R.

Sault Ste. Marie

St. Croix R.

Chippewa R.

Menominee R.

St. Ignace

Ottawa R.

L. Nipissing

Montreal

Ft. Le Sueur

Wisconsin R.

Wolf R.

Straits of Mackinac
Ft. Michilimackinac

Georgian Bay

St. Lawrence R.

Ft. La Baye

Butte des Morts

Green Bay

Fox R.

L. Michigan

L. Huron

Ste. Marie des Hurons

HURON

Ft. Frontenac

Ft. St. Nicolas

Mississippi R.

L. Ontario

Ft. Oswego

Ft. Niagara

IROQUOIS

Ft. Pontchartrain (Detroit)

L. St. Clair

L. Erie

Detail of the painting, "La Vérendrye," by Frederic Remington.

EMPIRES IN CONFLICT

The explorers, missionaries and fur traders who came to the Great Lakes region in the seventeenth century were French. They came in search of an overseas empire, Christian converts and wealth to strengthen the power of France's mercantile kingdom. Within three decades from the time Quebec was founded by Samuel de Champlain in 1608, the French had established control of the St. Lawrence River and stood in a strategic position to control the Great Lakes region.

Early developments in French-Indian relations cast Lake Superior in a role of key importance to the success of French efforts to dominate the new world. Champlain alienated the Iroquois when he befriended their longstanding enemies, the Huron Indians. Consequently, the Iroquois became bitter enemies of the French and took every opportunity to oppose them. The Iroquois allied themselves first with the Dutch and then with the British, who supplied them with firearms. The Iroquois' strength in the lower Great Lakes country made them a substantial military force and allowed them to uproot and dominate local tribes. The French tried in several ways to overcome the Indians' hostility. One plan was to convert the Iroquois to Christianity; another was to counterbalance Iroquois strength by making allies of the Hurons, whose territory lay to the north of the Iroquois. Neither plan met with much success, and the early exploration, missionary and fur trading ventures of the French shifted northward toward Lake Superior away from the Iroquois. Thus, exploration of Lakes Michigan, Erie and Ontario didn't come until years later.

By 1623 Etienne Brulé and his companion, Grenoble, had discovered Lake Superior and the passageway of rapid waters now known as Sault Ste. Marie. Brulé may also have discovered a fur trading route from Lake Superior to the Mississippi, utilizing the Brule and St. Croix Rivers in present-day northwestern Wisconsin. However, credit for the discovery of this route usually goes to Daniel Greysolon, Sieur du Lhut, who used it a half-century later.

The French fashioned a map of Lake Superior sometime before 1658. The first Frenchmen to write in detail about their travels on Lake Superior were Médart Chouart des Groseilliers and Pierre Esprit Radisson. Groseilliers and Radisson stole away from Trois-Rivières (between Quebec and Montreal) for a trip west in 1659. They did not get the required licenses, permission to make the trip, or a representative of the French government to go with them, all of which had repercussions later. Their two-year travels, which Radisson later recorded, took them to Sault Ste. Marie and along the southern shore of Lake Superior to Chequamegon Bay. There they built a small dwelling, which is commemorated today at a roadside park in Ashland, Wisconsin (see entry 104). The two moved inland for a while, probably to Lac Court Oreilles in Sawyer County, Wisconsin, and then returned to the bay and probably explored the Pigeon River. Gooseberry State Park and the Gooseberry River in Minnesota are named in honor of Groseilliers. ("Gooseberry" was the British "translation" of Groseilliers' name—see entry 5).

The two men returned to Montreal and Quebec with beaver pelts and stories of possibilities for a rich fur trade. They urged French authorities to establish fur trade through the Hudson Bay marketing outlet and to abandon the hazardous Iroquois-threatened route through the Great Lakes and the St. Lawrence River. French authorities, displeased with the travelers for making an unauthorized trip, ignored their advice. Annoyed, Radisson and Groseilliers went to the British with their tales of riches in furs and became instrumental in founding the Hudson's Bay Company, whose aggressive competition in the fur trade ultimately contributed to the fall of New France.

Meanwhile French explorers, missionaries and fur traders, lured by the wealth of furs reported by Radisson and Groseilliers, quickly moved into the Lake Superior area. In the 1660s, two prominent French explorers of the lake were Louis Jolliet and Jean Péré. During the same decade, French Jesuit missionaries coming to Superior included René Ménard, Claude Jean Allouez and Father Marquette. So vigorously did the Jesuits pursue their work that by 1680 their missions encircled Lake Superior. Keweenaw Bay, Michigan; Chequamegon Bay, Wisconsin; Duluth, Minnesota; and Lake Nipigon and Sault St. Marie, Ontario were all sites of early missions. Nevertheless, the Jesuits were engaged in a discouraging business—for the Chippewa were difficult to convert.

Until 1668 Chequamegon Bay was the focal point for the French fur trade on Lake Superior. Then fur trading patterns shifted from Lake Superior to Green Bay. The change came largely as the result of a peaceful, but temporary, agreement between the French and the Iroquois in 1667.

In the early 1670s, the French became worried about the growing strength of the British Hudson's Bay Company, which had been founded in 1670. They were also concerned about the growing English colonies lying to the south of New France along the Atlantic Seaboard from Massachusetts to Virginia. The French felt they needed to strengthen their

Father Hennipen's 1698 map of the Great Lakes.

hold on the Great Lakes country and establish stronger claims westward and southward if they were to successfully guard against the British bid for North America. This feeling led to the elaborate ceremony at Sault Ste. Marie in 1671—the Ceremony of Saint Lusson— that proclaimed that all the interior of North America belonged to the King of France (see entry 46-47).

In an attempt to strengthen the French position in the Great Lakes area, Daniel Greysolon, Sieur du Lhut, was sent to Lake Superior in 1678 to establish peace and friendship with the various Indian tribes. His travels took him to Sault Ste. Marie, to the present site of Duluth and through the Brule-St. Croix route to the Mississippi River. Du Lhut hoped to discover a northwest passage and the sea to the west, but his dreams were continually frustrated. He was repeatedly called back east to untangle troubled Indian relationships and to help repel the Iroquois. In the 1680s his travels led him to the Kaministikwia River, near the site of present-day Thunder Bay where he made an alliance with the Assiniboin and the Cree Indians. There he built a supply and trading post (see entry 26).

When Great Britain and France went to war in 1689, Britain's allies, the Iroquois, attacked New France. The French fur trade on Lake Superior had already suffered badly from English competition, and by the close of the 1680s, English traders had penetrated to the Straits of Mackinac. The French tried to reestablish lost ground in 1693 when they sent Pierre Le Sueur, instead of the ailing du Lhut, to Lake Superior to reopen the fur trade routes and form an alliance with the Sioux. Le Sueur established posts at La Pointe on the south shore of Madeline Island and at the mouth of the St. Croix River on the Mississippi River. He succeeded in making an alliance with the Sioux. Perhaps he was too successful, for in 1696, in response to ruinously low fur prices, Louis XIV revoked all fur-trading licenses and prohibited traders from taking trade goods into the west. For ten years the west was deserted by French traders.

This marked the beginning of the end of French fur trade and exploration. In 1713 the Treaty of Utrecht was signed, settling the British-French conflict known as Queen Anne's War. By the terms of the treaty, the French relinquished claim to Acadia (Nova Scotia and part of New Brunswick), Newfoundland and Hudson Bay. They also recognized the Iroquois as British subjects and the Iroquois empire as British domain.

Following the settlement, the French again made an effort to assert their authority in the Lake Superior area by reestablishing three posts—at La Point on Madeline Island and at

Fort Kaministikwia and Lake Nipigon in present-day Ontario. At Nipigon, the last of the French explorers, Sieur de la Vérendrye, learned from an Indian associate of a route which he believed to be the northwest passage. In 1731 Vérendrye started westward from Grand Portage on an expedition that opened the plains fur trade to the French and placed them in competition with the Hudson's Bay Company in yet another area. This was the last of the great French explorations because the French regime, riddled with graft and moral decay, fell to the British in 1763. La Point yielded to the British in 1759 and Fort Kaministikwia, Detroit, Mackinac and Green Bay soon followed suit.

The lure of a new empire and the beaver pelts, so highly prized in the European market, led to the French-British contest on Lake Superior. While hindsight is rather useless, one wonders how the contest between Britain and France would have ended had the French listened to the advice of Radisson and Groseilliers in 1659 instead of punishing them for trading without a license and causing them to side with the British.

Frederic Remington's painting, "Radisson and Groseilliers," first appeared in *Collier's Weekly* **in 1906.**

Sault Ste. Marie: Ontario & Michigan

Saute Ste. Marie locks, 1875.

" A very violent current of waters from Lake Superior...checked by a great number of rocks... [and forming] a dangerous cascade of half a league in width, all these waters descending and plunging headlong together, as by the flight of stairs, over the rocks which bar the whole river."

Father Claude Dablon so described Sault Ste. Marie, then known as Sainte Marie du Sault, in the *Jesuit Relation* of 1669-70. By then, more than a few Frenchmen had already visited the Sault in pursuit of the fur trade and lured by the possibility of finding a water route through the North American continent —

Etienne Brule, perhaps, in 1618 and 1621, Jean Nicolet in 1634, Radisson and Groseilliers in 1656. Not later than 1668, Fathers Louis Nicolas and Jacques Marquette established a Jesuit mission there, the first Euro-American settlement in the present state of Michigan.

Trying to head off the competition from British fur traders of the Hudson's Bay Company and recognizing the Sault's strategic potential in controlling the mid-continent, the French staged an elaborate ceremony here in 1671. This Pageant of Saint Lusson included a special envoy of Louis XIV, four Jesuit fathers and Indian representatives from 14 tribes.

The object of the ceremony was to proclaim legal possession of all territory drained by the Great Lakes in the name of the king of France and to affirm friendship between the French and the Indians.

The French regime at the Sault had its ups and downs. A massacre and fire at the Sault mission in 1674 led to the building of a second mission. After 1700 the French placed greater emphasis on Detroit and less on Michilimackinac (at the nearby Straits of Mackinac) and the Sault.

To meet the growing British threat, they belatedly built a fort at the Sault in 1751. The British occupied it a decade later. When the fort burned in 1762, the British withdrew to Fort Michilimackinac. The years of British control of the area were characterized by intense competition among the many traders for furs and for the abundant supplies of whitefish in the waters of the Sault.

Entering into that competition came the newly-established North West Company, locating first on the American side of the Sault. The 1783 decision to establish the Canadian-U.S. boundary through the middle of Lakes Superior and Huron led the North West Company to move to the Canadian side. There in 1797-98, the company built a small canal with a 38-foot lock so canoes and bateaux could negotiate around the river's rapids. The North West Company post on the north side of the rapids marked the beginning of the Canadian Sault settlement. Before that, the area had not been considered a desirable place for settlement because of the swamps.

During the War of 1812 the Americans pillaged and burned the North West Company property, as well as that of other Canadian traders on both sides of the Sault. In 1816 the American Fur Company established a post on the American side. The North West Company, soon to amalgamate with the Hudson's Bay Company, rebuilt their operation on the Canadian side.

Upon the recommendation of General Cass, work began on Fort Brady in 1821 to establish American authority, particularly among the Indians who were still loyal to the British. During the first half of the nineteenth century the two Saults remained focal points for the fur trade and for the transshipment of goods into and out of Lake Superior. They were also a center of mission activity for Protestants and Catholics alike.

On the American side was the fort and an Indian Agency, where Henry Schoolcraft served. In 1848 Louis Agassiz's expedition found the American Sault a straggling village of perhaps 300 persons—largely transient traders, voyageurs, Indians and miners waiting for employment.

Many recognized the need for a canal around the rapids of St. Mary's River in the early phases of the fur trade, but canal construction did not become a matter of public policy until the canal building craze of the 1830s.

After Michigan passed from territorial status to statehood in 1836, canal advocates marshalled their forces and got the state legislature to approve the construction of a canal at the Sault. A survey was undertaken in 1837 but the state effort ended in failure two years later. In the 1840s, when the copper and iron wealth of the Upper Peninsula became apparent, pressures from the mining interests bolstered interest in a canal. It was very inconvenient to haul heavy loads of ore, not to mention steamboats and other craft, overland around the rapids.

Fishing in the turbulent waters of St. Mary's River, 1898.

Michigan pressed Congress for help with canal construction. Finally in 1852, federal legislation passed, providing a right-of-way for the canal. The government also granted Michigan three-quarters of a million acres of federal land that the state could sell to help cover construction costs for the canal. The original canal was completed in 1855 at a cost of about $1,000,000. It has since been repeatedly enlarged and improved. The canal was transferred to the United States government in 1881 because of its importance to the national economy and because of the high costs of maintaining and operating it.

The Canadians decided to build their own canal after the American government refused to permit them to transport troops westward through the canal to quell the Riel rebellion of 1870. Construction on the Canadian canal began in 1887 and finished in 1895.

During the late nineteenth century, the two Saults remained basically shipping points and depended upon the wealth that came from the operation of the canals—loads of ore, grain and timber passed southeastward and coal, machinery and general freight traveled northwestward. Today, more tonnage passes through the Sault canals than through any other canal in the world.

Lying off the beaten path of settlement, the two Saults began to develop industrially only at the turn of the century. The Canadian side developed first as part of the dream of a Maine promoter, Francis Hector Clergue, who visited Sault Ste. Marie in 1894 in search of potential hydroelectric sites.

Impressed with the forest and mineral wealth of the area, as well as its hydro potential, he bought an unfinished power generating canal and built a very large pulp mill there. Clergue invested heavily in iron mines in the Michipicoten District—principally the Helen mine—and in mines located near Sudbury, Canada. He built a railroad connecting the Helen mine with Michipicoten Harbor, where freighters were loaded with ore destined for his steel mill at Sault Ste. Marie.

Clergue's plans included the American Sault, as well. There he bought rights to a power canal and developed a hydroelectric plant before the need for its generating capacity clearly existed. An elaborate campaign, begun at the turn of the century to attract American and Canadian investors for Clergue's projects, failed and so did his industrial empire in 1904. From Clergue's tangled assets Sir James Dunn eventually developed the successful Algoma Steel Corporation.

The Canadian Sault has outstripped the American side in industrial development. Steel, chemicals, paper, lumber, veneer and hydroelectric plants dominate the manufacturing community there. On the American side, a calcium carbide manufacturing plant, a marine and machine company, a leather products plant, woolen mills and hydroelectric installations give the community economic vitality beyond that which is derived from handling traffic through the canal.

Today, the American and Canadian locks permit toll-free passage to and from Lake Superior for ships

from all ports of the world. The most recent American-built lock is the Poe lock, completed in 1969, to replace a smaller Poe lock completed in 1896. Passage through the lock, which compensates for a water level difference of 22 feet between Lake Superior and Lake Huron, takes about 15 minutes.

A railroad bridge was built across the St. Mary's River in 1888 but automobile traffic relied on ferry transportation until 1962 when the International Bridge, financed by both governments, was completed. It extends across the river in a series of eight arch and truss bridges. The rapids from which the cities got their name may still be seen in the river, although they are only half as wide as they once were, due to the construction of the canals and locks.

SAULT STE. MARIE, ONTARIO
SITES OF INTEREST

The different street levels in downtown Sault Ste. Marie illustrate the terracing effect caused by changes in Great Lakes shoreline levels over time. As a result, there are abrupt differences in street levels.

Fish Hatchery. One mile east of Landslide Road, east of Hiawatha Park. A trout-rearing station.

Weyerhaeuser Company, People's Road. Plant tours Monday-Friday, minimum age 12 years. ($)

Museum of Early Sault History, 2nd Floor, Armory Building, 375 Pint St. Displays by the Sault Ste. Marie Historical Society and artifacts retrieved by divers from the St. Mary's River and Lake Superior are housed here. The 49th Field Regiment, Royal Canadian Artillery displays its military history here also. Open Wednesday afternoons.

Bellevue Park, 41 Lake Street. The park and gardens on the St. Mary's River provide a beautiful place to picnic and relax.

Sault Locks boat trips may be enjoyed aboard CHIEF SHINGWAUK and LE VOYAGEUR. ($)

Old Stone House, 31 Queen Street East. Built by Charles Oakes Ermatinger in 1814, the house has been restored. Ermatinger, an official of the North West Company, married the daughter of Chief Catawabeta of the Chippewa tribe. The old stone house was frequently the scene of caribou dinners attended by company officials, fur trappers and soldiers from Fort Brady. A museum of the fur trade in the area has been installed in some of the rooms. Open daily, June 1-September 30.

The tour boat, LE VOYAGEUR, takes visitors through the locks.

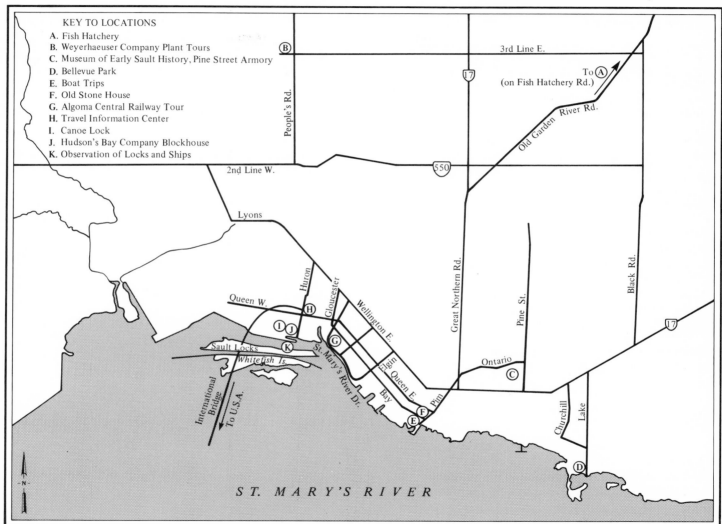

KEY TO LOCATIONS
A. Fish Hatchery
B. Weyerhaeuser Company Plant Tours
C. Museum of Early Sault History, Pine Street Armory
D. Bellevue Park
E. Boat Trips
F. Old Stone House
G. Algoma Central Railway Tour
H. Travel Information Center
I. Canoe Lock
J. Hudson's Bay Company Blockhouse
K. Observation of Locks and Ships

ST. MARY'S RIVER

Algoma Central Railway Tour to Agawa Canyon.
This all-day excursion includes a two-hour stop at
a canyon picnic ground in beautiful Canadian wilderness country. Each season has its own particular
contribution to make to the scenic beauty of this
trip. Obtain tickets from Algoma Passenger Center,
Bay Street. Operates daily from late May to early
October.

Canoe Lock, located on the Abitibi Paper Company
grounds, is a restoration of a portion of the lock built
by the North West Company fur traders from 1797-

Restored portion of North West Company canoe lock.

98. A plaque commemorates the destruction of the original lock by American soldiers during the War of 1812.

Hudson's Bay Company Blockhouse, located near the Canoe Lock. An interesting example of an historic structure that has undergone many changes, "blockhouse" is really a misnomer. Originally built by the North West Company (probably in 1819) as a magazine, it has massive stone walls and no windows. When Francis H. Clergue began industrial developments here in the late nineteenth century, he had the building altered and inserted windows. It became the first story of a new structure, which was topped with a log cabin-type second story. Calling it "the block house," Clergue used it to lavishly entertain prospective investors. As a result it is often erroneously referred to as the Hudson's Bay Company's original blockhouse. Although remnants of the North West Company-Hudson's Bay Company post still stood in the late nineteenth century, all of the buildings, except for this magazine, were razed to make room for industrial development.

Observation of locks and ships. A fascinating way to spend an afternoon is to watch ships passing through the Canadian or American locks. A good observation spot for the Canadian lock can be reached by taking Hy 17 B to the Bridge Plaza and turning south on Huron Street to the lock. St. Mary's Rapids can also be seen from here. Maps and photographs depicting the history and construction of the Canadian Lock and Canal are displayed in the Administrative Building.

Lake Superior Corporation, created at turn of century.

SAULT STE. MARIE, MICHIGAN

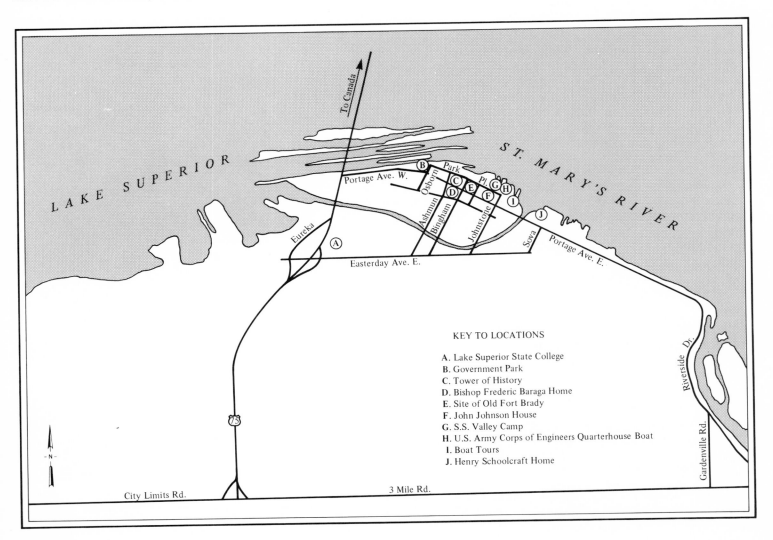

LAKE SUPERIOR

To Canada

ST. MARY'S RIVER

Portage Ave. W.

Osborn

Park

Pl

Ashmun

Bingham

Johnstone

Sowa

Portage Ave. E.

Eureka

Easterday Ave. E.

Riverside Dr.

Gardenville Rd.

75

City Limits Rd.

3 Mile Rd.

KEY TO LOCATIONS

A. Lake Superior State College
B. Government Park
C. Tower of History
D. Bishop Frederic Baraga Home
E. Site of Old Fort Brady
F. John Johnson House
G. S.S. Valley Camp
H. U.S. Army Corps of Engineers Quarterhouse Boat
I. Boat Tours
J. Henry Schoolcraft Home

SAULT STE. MARIE, MICHIGAN
SITES OF INTEREST

American Locks. The viewing area for the American locks may be reached from Route I-75 by exiting on Easterday Avenue, going east to South Ashmun to Portage Avenue and east to the locks.

Government Park, operated by the U.S. Army Corps of Engineers, has an observation deck for daily viewing of lock operations. At the information center the visitor can watch a film showing the many changes that have occurred in the American locks since the original was built in 1855. Scale models of the locks are also on display. The Poe lock on the south channel was rebuilt in 1969, making it the only lock large enough to accommodate today's 1,000-foot "super lakers."

Tower of History, 326 East Portage Avenue. Standing across the street from the Baraga home, this 210-foot, 21-story tower affords a fine view of the Sault locks, the cities, the lake and the surrounding country. The lobby contains a variety of displays relating to the history of Sault Ste. Marie. Open daily, May-September. ($)

Bishop Frederic Baraga's Home, 305 East Portage Avenue. Bishop Baraga resided at the Sault from 1853 until the seat of the diocese was moved to Marquette in 1866. He occupied this home, which was built in 1860 and has been restored. Open daily May-September.

Old Fort Brady*. The United States Army established the fort in 1822 on a site bounded now by Portage Avenue, Brady Street, Bingham Street and the C.O.E. Plaza. The initial purpose of the fort was to protect the area and to impress the Indians and wean them from their British friendships. In the summer of 1977, Michigan State University students completed a two-year archaeological study of the old fort site during which they located many artifacts. A similar project in 1967 had established the dimensions of the fort's exterior walls.

Bishop Frederic Baraga.

New Fort Brady*. The new fort was built on the bluffs overlooking Sault Ste. Marie in 1892. The state of Michigan acquired the fort buildings and developed them as the Sault Ste. Marie branch of Michigan Technological University. Instruction began there in 1946. In 1968 this school became a separate, undergraduate degree-granting institution, Lake Superior State College. The visitor can see the buildings on campus at Easterday Avenue.

John Johnston House*, **415 Park Place**. John Johnston built this one and a half story log home in 1794. Johnston, agent for Montreal fur traders Todd, McGill and Company, came to the Sault from La Pointe. Fire destroyed the home in 1814 and it was rebuilt the following year. Johnston, who married a Chippewa Indian chief's daughter, retained his allegiance to the British until the Americans firmly established their authority at the Sault. Then,

Henry Schoolcraft Home.

bowing to the inevitable, this successful British-Canadian fur trader and patriarch of the American Sault community recognized American authority. Johnston entertained General Cass's expedition in his home and Johnston's daughter, Jane, became the wife of one of the expedition members—Henry Schoolcraft. Married in 1823, the couple occupied an addition to her father's house for four years.

S.S. Valley Camp*, built in 1917 as the LOUIS W. HILL, had its name changed in 1955. In its 50 years of service, the ship carried over 16 million tons of cargo. It is now a floating marine museum which may be toured by the public. The No. 3 hold contains interesting historical exhibits. Located off East Portage Avenue. ($)

U.S. Army Corps of Engineers Quarterhouse Boat, berthed next to the VALLEY CAMP, was used as headquarters by engineers working on marine projects. Visitors may tour the boat. Open May-September. ($)

Boat Tours. Boat tours through the locks can be arranged on both the Michigan and Canadian sides of the river.

Henry Schoolcraft Home*, 705 East Portage Avenue. Plans call for restoration of this home, now on the grounds of the Edison Power Company. This Indian Agency House was completed in 1827. Henry Schoolcraft, a member of General Lewis Cass's expedition in 1820 to explore the Michigan Territory, became interested in the Indians living in the area and was appointed U.S. Indian Agent. His

St. Mary's Falls canal.

contemporaries considered him an authority on Indians and his research material was adapted by Longfellow for the famous poem, "The Song of Hiawatha."

Iroquois Point Lighthouse.

48. BAY MILLS INDIAN RESERVATION

[Sugar Island, southeast of Sault Ste. Marie and north of Bay Mills on Hy 221]

The original Bay Mills Reservation for a Chippewa Indian community was purchased by the Methodist Mission Society and then acquired by the federal government in accordance with the treaty of July 1, 1855. Lands were added to the reservation under terms of the Indian Reorganization Act of 1934. Today the reservation includes 2,189 acres and 760 Indians live there or nearby. Tribal headquarters are at Brimley.

49. BRIMLEY STATE PARK

[Michigan, Hy M 221, (P-C-F-B-S)]

A nice beach borders Whitefish Bay, although Lake Superior is usually too cold for swimming.

50. BRIMLEY

[Take Brimley Road from Hy 28]

From Lake Shore Road, four miles west of Brimley, visitors may view an old Indian burial ground. Small, wooden house-like structures cover the graves, each with an opening at one end to allow the passage of spirits. Visitors are not encouraged to enter the burial ground.

51. IROQUOIS POINT LIGHTHOUSE

[Six miles northwest of Brimley]

Because the Chippewa defeated the Iroquois in a battle fought here in 1662, this point of land is called Iroquois Point. Since then, the point has served as a well-known landmark for lake travelers—Indians, missionaries, fur traders, crews of ore and cargo vessels, and passengers on holiday cruise ships. The first lighthouse was built on Iroquois Point in 1857 when the first ore-laden vessels passed by on their way through the Upper St. Mary's River and the newly opened locks at Sault Ste. Marie. A taller lighthouse, with attached quarters for the keeper and his family, replaced the old one in 1870 and saw many years of service. But when Canada installed an automatic light on the Gros Cap shore in 1962, the Iroquois Point Lighthouse was no longer necessary. The property was then transferred to the U.S. Forest Service which has made the grounds of the lighthouse available for picnics. Unfortunately, vandals have badly damaged the old lighthouse and residence.

52. PENDILLS CREEK
NATIONAL FISH HATCHERY

[North of Hy 28 in Hiawatha National Forest]

One of three federal lake trout hatcheries in this area, the hatchery was established to replenish lake trout populations in the Great Lakes. Four million lake trout fingerlings are planted in the lakes yearly and this has had a tremendous effect on increasing the popularity of Great Lakes sport fishing.

53. HIAWATHA NATIONAL FOREST

(P-H-C)

Established in 1931, Hiawatha National Forest contains over 860,000 acres of land. Its timber provides an important resource for the lumber and paper industries, but the vacationer will also appreciate its charms. There are opportunities for hiking, picnicking and camping. The forest is divided into two sections separated by Michigan state forests. Hiawatha National Forest also includes Round and Government Islands in Lake Huron. Headquarters are in Escanaba, Michigan.

54. TAHQUAMENON FALLS STATE PARK AND LOWER TAHQUAMENON FALLS STATE PARK

[Hy M 123, (P-H-C-F-B-S)]

Once part of a vast wilderness, this park extends into both Luce and Chippewa Counties. In this very scenic area are the breathtaking Upper and Lower Falls (both reached via Hy M 123). The 200-foot wide Upper Falls drops a spectacular 40 feet into the Tahquamenon River. The visitor can view the Upper Falls on an excursion boat which picks up passengers at Slater's Landing, ten miles north of Hulbert off M 28, or on a narrow-gauge railroad which leaves from Soo Junction. Lower Tahquamenon Falls, also on Hy M 123, consists of a series of short drops and rapids. Approaching by rowboat, many visitors enjoy swimming in the shallow river beneath the rapids. Picnicking and camping facilities are nearby. The Rivermouth Unit of the park on Whitefish Bay, 4-1/2 miles north of Paradise, also offers camping facilities.

55. WHITEFISH POINT LIGHTHOUSE*

[11 miles north of Paradise]

Believed to be the oldest active light on Lake Superior, Whitefish Point Lighthouse dates from 1849. The light, housed in a 75-foot cylindrical iron tower, has been automated with fog signal and radio beacon since 1971. There is a keeper's dwelling as well.

Vermillion Point, about 40 miles west of Whitefish Point, was the location of a U.S. Lifesaving Station.

Lake Superior whitefish and trout, circa 1885.

It was established in 1876, after four schooners sank off the point during one terrible storm. A crew of six manned the station, the number needed to pull the oars of the big lifesaving boat. Until three more lifesaving stations were established in

1881, the only inhabitants of the Michigan shore between Whitefish Point and Grand Marais were the crew at Vermillion Point. Because of its isolated location, they called it "the loneliest place in America." Their presence, however, many times meant the saving of lives which would otherwise have been lost. The U.S. Coast Guard has now taken over the work of the Lifesaving Service.

On Whitefish Bay, opposite Whitefish Point, the ore carrier EDMUND FITZGERALD tragically sank during an intense storm the night of November 10, 1975. The 729-foot long ship went down in 500 feet of water and the entire crew of 29 was lost—there was no time for rescue operations of any type. Instances such as the FITZGERALD sinking have made Great Lakes sailors treat storms on Lake Superior with respect.

56. MUSKALLONGE LAKE STATE PARK

[Off M 123, 27 miles north of Newberry, (P-C-F-B-S)]

Seasoned campers choose this park, one of the wildest areas in the state of Michigan.

57. SENEY NATIONAL WILDLIFE REFUGE

[Hy 77, Germfask]

The Fish and Wildlife Service of the U.S. Department of the Interior established this refuge in 1935, the purpose of which is to restore wildlife habitat and protect waterfowl. A visitors' center offers interpretive displays and there are guided auto tours in summer, a nature trail and a picnic site. Geese, ducks, cranes, eagles, grouse and pileated woodpeckers frequent the area.

58. GRAND MARAIS

[Junction of Routes 77 and Hy 58]

A fine harbor of refuge, Grand Marais was a commercial fishing center first and later a lumbering village. In the vocabulary of the French voyageurs, Marais meant placid, protected cove or bay—a place of refuge. They also gave this name to another location on Lake Superior, a protected harbor in Minnesota.

One mile west of town begins the Pictured Rocks National Lakeshore. Grand Sable Falls and Grand Sable Dunes, which extend for seven miles from Lake Superior inland to Grand Sable Lake, are located here.

59. KINGSTON PLAIN

[Hy 58 near Au Sable Point]

Huge tree stumps remaining here give testimony to the cuts of the early logging days. Logs slid down the Devil's Slide, a huge sand dune, to waiting rafts which carried them nine miles across Lake Superior to the mills at Grand Marais. The log slide is still visible today.

Exploring Pictured Rocks cavern by rowboat, late nineteenth century.

60. PICTURED ROCKS
NATIONAL LAKESHORE

[Accessible from Hys 77 and 28 (P-H-C-S)]

The Pictured Rocks are comprised of a layer of soft sandstone capped with hard dolomite forms.

Mineral seepage has painted the rocks in various colors: iron shows up red; copper, blue and green; and limestone, white. The viewer can easily detect various "pictures" in the coloration on the rocks, and the wind and waves of Lake Superior have worked on the cliffs to form lovely caves and arches in the rocks as well.

A boat cruise offers the best opportunity to view the 15 miles of multicolored sandstone cliffs from which the National Lakeshore takes its name. Cruise boats leave the dock at Munising several times daily in summer.

The Au Sable Lighthouse complex, built on Au Sable Point in 1874, serves as headquarters for the Pictured Rocks National Lakeshore. Ore carriers found navigation around the point hazardous because thick fog often made the sandstone formations jutting out of the water invisible.

The completion of the light made their progress safer, but the area around Au Sable Point still posed many dangers. Telephone lines installed in 1897 which connected the lighthouse keeper with the life-saving station at Whitefish Point were a great boon to ships in trouble. The light was automated in 1958 and the land and buildings turned over to the National Park Service.

Au Sable Light is being restored by the Pictured Rocks National Lakeshore, which will open an historical interpretation center there by 1982. In the meantime, the park rangers conduct interpretive and campfire programs daily throughout the summer. The park has miles of sandy beaches, famous for their agate treasures, and hiking trails wind through the woods atop the bluffs. Many picturesque waterfalls near Munising invite the traveler. Among them are Tannery Falls one mile east; Alger Falls one mile south; Munising Falls 1.5 miles northeast; and Miners Falls eight miles northeast of Munising.

Excursion boat, Pictured Rocks National Lakeshore.

61. MUNISING

[Hy 28]

Facing Grand Island and ringed by hills on three sides, the site of Munising was a favorite camping place of the Chippewa Indians for centuries before white settlements penetrated Michigan's Upper Peninsula.

During the 1850s speculators platted the town, but no real development occurred until Peter White, a prominent leader in the development of Marquette, constructed a blast furnace there in 1867. Efforts to manufacture charcoal iron failed a decade later, but with the building of a tannery and several sawmills, Munising underwent a second boom in the 1890s. The village quickly developed and in 1919 became an incorporated city. Today, Munising's economic vitality comes chiefly from the manufacture of wooden ware, paper and other wood products, made possible by the surrounding forests' resources.

Alger County Historical Society operates two museum sites in Munising. One, at 203 West Onota Street, is the Lobb House* built in 1907 by Elizabeth Lobb, a prominent business woman with investments in an iron mine and brickyard. The lavish interior in-

cluded oak paneling and parquet bordered floors. The home is open afternoons, Monday to Friday.

Behind the courthouse, at the corner of Varnum and Park Streets, stands an 1840 cabin built by Alger County's first white settler, Abraham Williams. It was moved to its present site from Grand Island, where Williams operated a trading post. Containing exhibits of the mid-1800s, the cabin is open afternoons, Monday to Friday. Other Munising sites include a Kimberly-Clark Paper Mill, which conducts guided tours in summer, Monday to Friday. Pictured Rocks boat tours leave from the town dock.

Alger County Historical Museum, Munising.

Grand Island cabin, built by first white settler as a trading post, circa 1840.

62.   GRAND ISLAND

[Visible from Hy 28]

A short distance off shore, west of Munising, lies Grand Island. Named by the voyageurs, this island became the site of a minor fishery run by the American Fur Company. Some evidence of the island's early use in the fur trade remains today.

However, the Cleveland-Cliffs Iron Company owns the island and it is not generally open to visitors.

63.   MUNISING TO MARQUETTE

Along this route, Hy 28 runs very close to the Lake Superior shore, offering fine vistas for the traveler. There are also a number of places where you can walk down to the lakeshore.

64. BAY FURNACE PARK*

[Hy M 28, just west of Christmas]

The Bay Furnace Company built one single stack blast furnace and six charcoal kilns here in 1870. Most of the 20,000 acres of surrounding hardwood forest trees were cut and converted into charcoal to be used for fuel by the company. In 1877 the community of Onota, which had developed around the iron-making operations, was entirely destroyed by fire. Of the Bay Furnace facilities, only a portion of the stack remained.

In 1940 the U.S. Forest Service reforested a portion of the land and developed it for Bay Furnace Park. A sign in the park explains the pig iron production process and the Forest Service hopes to complete more restoration work here to preserve these remnants of the iron-making industry.

Smelting furnace, Bay Furnace Park.

65. STANNARD ROCK LIGHTHOUSE*

[40 miles northeast of Marquette]

Although not much bigger than a fisherman's dory, Stannard Rock marks one of the most dangerous reefs in Lake Superior. It was named for Captain Charles C. Stannard, who discovered it in 1835 while skippering the newly-launched schooner JOHN JACOB ASTOR for the American Fur Company. Special equipment was needed to build a lighthouse on Stannard Rock, 23 miles from land. The necessary equipment, used also to build the Spectacle Reef Lighthouse in the Straits of Mackinac in 1875, was moved to Huron Bay, and this site served as a construction depot. Adverse weather conditions made construction so difficult that the lighthouse was not completed until 1882 and cost $305,000. Keepers assigned to this light often found themselves isolated for entire seasons by storms. In 1961 the light became automated and today is visible for

Stannard Rock Lighthouse.

18 miles. The lighthouse also has automated weather reporting equipment.

66. MARQUETTE

[Hy 28 and 41]

Philo Everett, looking for mineral wealth, led a party of speculators from Jackson, Michigan into the Upper Peninsula in 1845. On a day when Everett stayed behind, an Indian guide led the party to deposits of iron ore at what became the Jackson Mine at Negaunee. With the development of the mine, a forge was built on the lakeshore at the mouth of the Carp River and this was the beginning of the present city of Marquette.

After the completion of the Sault Canal, the first ore dock was built here in 1857 and Marquette became the first Lake Superior port from which iron ore was shipped to mills on the lower Great Lakes. For a time, Michigan ranked first in the Union in the manufacture of pig iron; at least 25 furnaces in Upper Michigan produced pig iron from Lake Superior ore. However, because the furnaces depended upon charcoal for fuel, they were abandoned when the timber supply was gone.

The demands of an industrializing economy and the technological advances in iron mining led to the early depletion of high grade surface ores in the area. A number of plants in the Upper Peninsula now pelletize and upgrade low grade iron ore through a process developed jointly in 1954 by the Ford Motor Company and the Cleveland-Cliffs Iron Company.

Jackson Pit Mine No. 1, 1860.

In addition to the iron mines, the quarrying of brown sandstone also attracted settlers to the Marquette area. Sandstone was used in many Marquette buildings and was also shipped to other cities.

Today, Marquette remains an important ore-shipping center and has become an important year-round resort area. Chemicals, foundry products, mining machinery, wood products and agriculture are other important contributers to its economic life.

MARQUETTE SITES OF INTEREST

St. Peter's Cathedral, 4th and Baraga Streets. This cathedral is built of brown Lake Superior sandstone. Its crypt holds the remains of Bishop Frederic Baraga, first bishop of the diocese of Marquette. The Bishop Baraga Association has been formed to recognize the life and work of this missionary priest.

Burt House, 220 Craig Street. John Burt was active in the early development of Marquette. The house, built in 1858 of sandstone from a nearby quarry, functioned as warehouse and office for the Burt Brothers Sandstone Quarry. One of the three rooms, which are furnished in original period pieces, has an open fireplace used for heating and cooking. Open daily in July and August. ($)

Statue of Father Marquette, Lakeside Park. Adjacent to the Chamber of Commerce building stands this replica of the statue by Gaetano Trentenove which was placed in Statuary Hall, Washington, D.C., in 1904. Financed by Marquette citizens of French descent, the original statue was unveiled in Marquette, Michigan in 1897.

Marquette County Historical Museum and John M. Longyear Research Library, 213 North Front Street. The gift of a former mayor, the museum and library offer a large amount of information about the region's history. Museum exhibits, covering mining, Indians and early settlers, have been planned to introduce the vacation visitor to local points of historical interest. Open Monday to Friday.

Marquette Statue dedication, 1897.

Marquette and Huron Mountain Railroad is now a tour train at Presque Isle.

Carp River Forge, County Road 492. There are plans to restore this old forge, one of the region's earliest. A marker on the site commemorates its historical importance.

The Mather Mine, Negaunee, offers surface mine tours on weekdays (minimum age, 12 years). An unusually large underground iron ore mine, Mather Mine "B" covers two square miles within the city limits of both Negaunee and Ishpeming. The ore varies in color from dull red to bluish gray. This mine, the region's last remaining underground mine, is scheduled to close in 1979. On Iron Street, in Negaunee, near the Lake Shore and Ishpeming Railroad tracks, a pyramid-shaped monument marks the spot where iron was first discovered in 1844.

Republic Mine, Republic, Hy 95. An open pit mining operation can be observed from this vantage point.

Presque Isle Park on Lake Superior. (P-H-C). A monument to the last of the Chippewa chiefs, Charles Kawbawgam, stands on Lake Shore Boulevard. He was buried here in 1902. On Presque Isle Point, an American flag was raised by members of Governor Lewis Cass's expedition when they explored the south shore of Lake Superior in 1820. Today, the visitor can observe the loading of taconite pellets onto ships here. The Lake Shore and Ishpeming dock is located near the entrance to Marquette City Park.

Marquette & Huron Mountain Railroad. A steam-powered engine leaves the depot at Presque Isle Station for a 15-mile ride through a scenic wilderness area. Operates daily from June 26 through Labor Day. ($)

Jackson Mine Museum, Hy 41 east of Negaunee. This privately owned and operated museum contains exhibits on iron mining in the Marquette range. Open daily May through October.

(Numbered entries continued on p. 101)

Presque Isle Point.

IRON MINING

Iron mining in the Lake Superior region dates back more than 125 years. Richly endowed with mineral resources, the region's economic vitality today depends on iron mining, much as it has in the past. Thirteen iron ore districts span the Michigan-Wisconsin-Minnesota-Ontario borders (see map). Of these, the Mesabi range in Minnesota is the number one producer. Lake Superior's iron deposits furnish 80 percent of all iron ore produced in the U.S. and 18 percent of iron ore produced in Canada.

The tapping of Ontario's Lake Superior iron ore deposits began at the end of the nineteenth century when Francis Clergue, an American entrepreneur, invested heavily in Michipicoten iron mining and developed a steel plant at Sault Ste. Marie, Ontario. Other Ontario iron mines are twentieth century ventures, like the Steep Rock Mine at Atikokan, which opened during World War II.

Iron mining in Michigan began in the Marquette range in 1844, after the discovery of iron ore deposits at the site of present-day Negaunee. This discovery is sometimes credited to Philo M. Everett but William A. Burt, inventor of the solar compass, actually discovered ore in the area at an earlier date. Everett exploited Burt's discovery and put the Jackson Mining Company, originally formed to mine copper, to work mining iron ore.

Transportation problems plagued these early mining ventures in Michigan. Prior to the completion of the Sault Ste. Marie Canal, companies built forges and smelted the ore close to the mine sites and then transported it to market. For many years, more than 25 blast furnaces operated in the Upper Peninsula, fueled by locally-made hardwood charcoal. But by 1860, large producers had started exporting their ore for smelting.

Railroads provided a transportation outlet for the iron ore. A railroad from the Marquette range to Lake Superior began operating in 1857, and the Chicago and Northwestern Railroad opened up the Menominee range in 1877. The Cleveland Iron Company built a modern dock in 1859 at Marquette where ships could take on ore directly from railroad cars. While the presence of iron ore was known in the Bessemer area of Michigan's Gogebic range in 1873, mining did not begin until a railroad into the district was completed in 1884.

Slovenian and Finnish miners, 1910.

The key to cheap water transportation of the ore southward was the Sault Ste. Marie Canal, which opened in 1855. Ore carriers could load up and travel from Marquette to the lower lake ports, principally Cleveland. From there, the ore could be shipped eastward. During the Civil War, abundant coal supplies in the lower Midwest were used to smelt and refine the ore right at these ports so that further shipping became unnecessary.

Until the 1870s, Michigan iron mining was a relatively simple quarrying operation. In the 1870s, as surface deposits became depleted, shaft mining replaced earlier techniques. Shaft mining was done with wooden ladders and bucket hoists. By 1900 the mining process had grown more complex with elevators, hoisting machinery, pumps, power drills and dynamite. This required large investments of capital which caused a consolidation of companies and the disappearance of the smaller operators.

Today Cleveland-Cliffs Corporation is the big mining operation in the Marquette range and Michigan's chief producer of iron ore. Its dominance stems from the successful use of "beneficiation" processes, which are used to convert leaner ores into a more concentrated form.

Until 1900, Michigan led the country in iron ore production. Shipments from the Upper Peninsula grew from 1,449 tons in 1855 to 114,401 tons in 1860. By early in the twentieth century, millions of tons were being produced. The enormous economic growth of the nation had created a heavy demand for Michigan iron to build ships, railroads, machinery, factories and skyscrapers. For the traveler of Michigan's Lake Superior shoreline, iron mining—past and present—is very evident in Marquette (see entry 66) and in the Ironwood-Hurley area (see entry 98).

Minnesota's Vermilion and Mesabi ranges were relative latecomers to the Superior iron ore industry. In the early nineteenth century, reports of iron ore in Minnesota repeatedly came to public attention. Henry Eames found ore, 50 to 60 feet thick, at Vermilion Lake after an 1865 exploration, requested by Minnesota's governor. Iron ore riches in the Mesabi range came to light in the 1870s, though initial findings had pointed to the Vermilion range as the most promising area for development.

The Minnesota Iron Company was incorporated in 1882, spurred by an 1881 Minnesota law (repealed 15 years later) that restricted tax on iron ore to one cent per ton, and by liberal federal land sale policies. The Soudan mine soon began operation and the mining boom was under way. In 1884 a railroad was built to Two Harbors, Minnesota from the mining town of Tower—named for Charlemagne Tower, one of the guiding spirits in the Minnesota Iron Company. In the same year, ore went from Tower to Two Harbors where it was shipped out on ore carriers (see entry 4). From this beginning, iron ore production in the Vermilion mushroomed. By 1890 almost 300 mining companies had been incorporated there.

In retrospect, this was just the beginning. In November 1890, the Merritt brothers, a Duluth pioneer's sons who were known as the "Seven Iron Men," confirmed the riches of the Mesabi range. This 137-square-mile expanse of ore proved to be the most important of all the Superior iron ore deposits. While control of the Mesabi's development eventually

IRON ORE DISTRICTS OF LAKE SUPERIOR

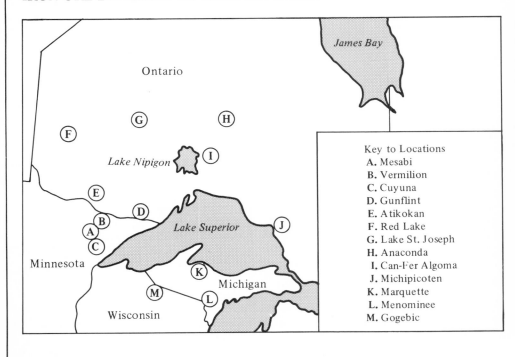

Key to Locations
A. Mesabi
B. Vermilion
C. Cuyuna
D. Gunflint
E. Atikokan
F. Red Lake
G. Lake St. Joseph
H. Anaconda
I. Can-Fer Algoma
J. Michipicoten
K. Marquette
L. Menominee
M. Gogebic

Mesabi Mine, 1920.

fell to others, the Merritt brothers did much to organize the industry. They formed the Mountain Iron Company, secured railroad connections from the ore beds to Duluth-Superior and were instrumental in constructing ore docks. In October, 1892, the first ore —4,245 tons—moved over the railroad to Duluth. However, the Merritts became financially overcommitted during the panic year of 1893 and lost their interests and control to John D. Rockefeller. Rockefeller and his colleagues were far better equipped than small operators like the Merritts, to handle the major capital investments that mining demanded.

In the 1890s Mesabi iron mining expanded tremendously. Along with Rockefeller, the financial leaders of the business were Andrew Carnegie, Henry W. Oliver, who had made a fortune in the farm implement business, and James J. Hill of the Great Northern Railroad. The New York financial magnate, J. Pierpont Morgan, organized the Carnegie, Rockefeller and Oliver interests into the U.S. Steel Corporation in 1901.

Near the turn of the century, Minnesota's great ore resources began to overshadow those of Michigan. In the 1890s, Minnesota's mines produced about 43 million tons of ore and in the next decade, about five times that much. By the early 1940s, in response to war-time demand for iron, production was more than 338 million tons.

Mesabi iron mining is an open pit operation. Great shovels are used to scoop up and load the ore into railroad cars for shipment to processing plants and, eventually, to the country's steel centers. In 1972, these shipments totalled more than 51 million tons. Future prospects are bright for the Mesabi surface mines—their wealth of ore promises to last for at least 200 years—but the future of underground mining operations in Minnesota's Vermilion range is less certain.

A look at iron mining in the Lake Superior area goes beyond company histories and production figures. Lake Superior itself played a vital role in shaping the iron industry in the Great Lakes area. It served as a great avenue for delivering ore to blast furnaces on the lower lakes. Without this highway for ore carriers, the iron industry might well have developed with refineries adjacent to the mines and this would have changed the whole character of the region. The ore boats make up an important chapter in the story of Lake Superior iron mining (see "Lake Superior's Ships," page 21).

Then, too, there were the workers. Thousands of skilled and unskilled people came to work in the iron mines—Americans from eastern mining communities, Cornishmen, Swedes, Italians, Slovenes, Croats, Romanians, Norwegians, Irish, Finns, Poles, Germans and French-Canadians. In 1900 at least half the people living in the Mesabi region were foreign-born. Their ethnic legacy lingers on, plainly visible in Superior iron mining country.

Also important to the success of the mining industry was direct encouragement from federal and state governments. Initially, mineral land was cheap and easy to acquire from the federal government. Then came state taxing policies that benefitted the mining businesses and government-sponsored research to solve their technical problems. More recently, states have underwritten attempts to discover new sources of ore and have provided special tax incentives, encouraging mining companies to experiment with taconite, a black magnetic iron-bearing ore that presents special problems in extraction and beneficiation.

Finally, iron mining operations have not escaped the land and water use questions that face other industries. The Mesabi range abuts the Superior National Forest (see entry 12) and the Gogebic range falls partially within the Chequamegon National Forest (see entry 107). The conflict between industrial development and environmental interests requires careful resolution to insure that the natural beauty of the Lake Superior country is preserved and, at the same time, that we make the most of the region's great natural wealth.

Loading ore at Bessemer mine, 1946.

67. HURON ISLANDS

[Three miles off the southern shore of Lake Superior]

A national refuge for double-crested cormorants, terns and herring gulls was established on the islands in 1938. It is operated by the U.S. Department of the Interior, Fish and Wildlife Service.

In 1868, the Huron Islands Lighthouse* was built onto a three-family dwelling on the northeast side of West Huron Island. The light, built on a granite outcropping 197 feet above the water, guided ships entering the Portage Ship Canal past hidden shoals. In addition to tending the light, crewmen manned a lifeboat station and stood ready to assist any ship in the area in trouble. Because it was not in an isolated location, however, the station did not have the full six-man crew found in a first class life-saving station. The light has been automated since 1972. It is not accessible to the public.

68. PEQUAMING

[Take Pequaming Road from Hy 41]

Pequaming, about ten miles north of L'Anse off Keweenaw Bay, started as a sawmill town in 1879. Charles Hebard patterned the town after an English country village. It was purchased in 1923 by Henry Ford, the founder of the Ford Motor Company, who was experimenting with theories on rural production and decentralization at several communities on Michigan's Upper Peninsula at that time.

Double-crested cormorant.

The mill, its docks, tugs, a scow and the town itself were bought to supply lumber for the production of Ford automobiles. In 1942, when wood was no longer used in building automobiles, Ford closed the town. Then in 1968, a group of Baraga County businessmen bought Pequaming, demolished many of the rotting buildings and made plans to sell the land for homesites. Some of the Ford structures, however, were left intact by Pequaming Properties, Inc., and visitors may drive by and see the old sawmill, the company store, Ford's summer bungalow, a few houses and a one-room schoolhouse.

69. CHIPPEWA INDIAN CEMETERY

[Five miles east of L'Anse]

This cemetery, begun about 1840, contains a number of Indian grave sites covered with small wooden houses made of pine lumber with shingle roofs and windows facing west. These were designed to protect grave sites from wolves and other wild animals. The last grave house was built in 1904. To locate this burial ground, drive east from L'Anse on Skanee Road to a gravel road marked Indian Cemetery Road. Turn right and continue to the end, where the road circles a pine-covered sandy hill.

70. ALBERTA

[Hy 41]

Henry Ford established Alberta, about ten miles south of L'Anse on Hy 41, as an experimental self-sufficient community in 1936. A model sawmill on the banks of Plumbago Creek employed the residents and produced 15,000 board feet of lumber daily. At least 12 families lived in homes built on land cleared from the dense forest and their children attended a village school modeled after one at Ford's Greenfield Village.

In 1954, Alberta was presented to Michigan Technological University for the Ford Forestry Center. Its facilities, including 4,000 acres of forest land, have become an outdoor laboratory for research and demonstration in forest management and wood utilization.

Indian cemetery near L'Anse.

Michigan: Keweenaw Peninsula

Replica of Father Frederic Baraga Chapel, Assinins.

71. L'ANSE

[Hy 41]

Father René Ménard, visiting this area in 1660, named the southern shore of the bay L'Anse de Ste. Therese, later shortened to L'Anse, meaning cove. It is believed that Ménard established a mission among the Ottawa Indians, locating his chapel at Pequaming, seven miles to the northeast. The L'Anse site served as a campground for French explorers, trappers and missionaries. Father Frederic Baraga began a mission here in 1843 on the western shore of the bay. Methodist missionaries frequented the eastern shore and prior to 1843 established a mission at the present site of Zeba.

By the late nineteenth century lumbering had become important in this area. Platted in 1871, the village of L'Anse became the county seat when Baraga County organized in 1875.

Father Baraga Statue near L'Anse.

Shrine of the Snowshoe Priest, one mile west of L'Anse on Hy 41 on the red rock bluffs.

An impressive statue of Father Baraga was erected here in 1972 to honor his missionary work. The 35-foot tall figure weighs four tons and is supported on laminated wooden beams rising from concrete tepees ten feet tall. These represent the five major missions started by Bishop Baraga. Made from materials furnished by the White Pine Mine of the Copper Range Mining Company, the striking figure, made of brass sheeting, picks up and reflects the sunlight. The statue overlooks Keweenaw Bay. For about ten miles from this point north on Hy 41, the traveler gets an excellent view of the bay.

72. JACOBSVILLE SANDSTONE

[Along Hy 41 between L'Anse and Baraga]

Exposed sections of the sandstone, prevalent in the Upper Peninsula, distinguish this area. At Jacobsville, near L'Anse, the rock appears reddish-brown; near Marquette the rock takes on a more brownish color. Sandstone was popular with architects for building use because it is easily cut and carved. However, the sandstone began to lose favor at the turn of the century when it was judged to be too highly colored for the current taste.

73. NORTH COUNTRY TRAIL

When the North Country Trail for cross-country skiing and backpacking is complete, it will link up with the Lewis and Clark Trail in North Dakota. This will form part of a 3,200-mile trail from

Vermont to the West Coast. The North Country Trail will cross the Huron Mountains east of L'Anse and continue through the Porcupine Mountains to the west.

74. BARAGA STATE PARK

[One mile south of Baraga, Hy 41, (P-H-C-F-B-S)]

This 60-acre, pleasantly wooded park is right on the shore of Keweenaw Bay.

75. SAND POINT BURIAL MOUNDS*

[Near Baraga, off Hy 41]

Sand Point is the location of a series of Indian burial mounds, dating probably from 1100 to 1300 A.D. Digs by the Michigan Archaeological Society and Western Michigan University have revealed artifacts and skeletons which may connect these sites with the Mississippian peoples. Steps have been taken to preserve the location.

76. KEWEENAW BAY RESERVATION

[Access from Hy 41]

This 13,750-acre Chippewa reservation, recognized by the treaty of 1854, is the largest Indian reservation in the state of Michigan. The tribe owns 1,610 acres, individual Indians own 8,124 acres, and the federal government owns 4,016 acres. The population numbers about 500. L'Anse Community College is located on the reservation and there is a pottery shop here that is also of interest to visitors.

(Numbered entries continued on p. 109)

Cross country skiing on Upper Michigan trails.

THE PIONEER MISSIONARIES

Of all the frontiersmen who braved the Lake Superior wilderness, none endured greater hardships and frustration nor showed greater devotion to their work than the missionaries. Theirs was the business of spreading Christianity in a sparsely-populated wilderness, accessible only by canoe in the warm months of summer and by dog sled, horse travois, snowshoes and skis during the long severe winter.

The diary of James Evans, a Canadian Methodist missionary, reveals the hardships involved in his record of a journey on Lake Superior from Sault Ste. Marie to Michipicoten late in the fall of 1838. He recounted one miserable day: "The day has been severely cold—our paddles and ores and canoe coated with ice, and when we landed our clothes and our loading were nearly an inch thick with ice, nor could we erect our tent until it had lain nearly an hour before the fire, but it's all over, thanks to God we are now warm on the fire side and by changing sides can keep comfortable."

The initial goal of these Christian missionaries was to convert the Indian population. It was an ambitious and extremely difficult task. The Jesuit fathers, who accompanied the French explorers and fur traders, established the first Indian missions in the seventeenth century. During this period of French domination on Lake Superior, several Jesuit missionaries were prominent—among them, René Ménard, Claude Jean Allouez and Jacques Marquette. By the late 1600s, centers of Jesuit mission activity included Keweenaw Bay and Chequamegon Bay, Fond du Lac (modern Duluth), the southeastern shore of Lake Nipigon and Sault Ste. Marie.

This French missionary work declined after the French lost control of the region in 1763. For a time, neither the British-Canadians nor the Americans had well-organized missionary activities in the Lake Superior region. But about 1820, mission work entered a new and vigorous era as Protestants joined the Catholic effort. Missionaries expanded their audience to include the white settlers in the Lake Superior area—fur traders, fishermen, miners, soldiers, farmers and lumber camp workers.

The Christian churches took their obligations to serve the sparsely-settled frontier areas very seriously. They worked hard to organize mission activities, raise funds for them and send pastors and priests into newly-developing regions. It was not unusual for one pastor

Father Baraga and Indian parishioners.

or priest to serve several congregations in different communities. Then, as settlements became larger, they established their own churches with resident pastors or priests.

Perhaps the most extraordinary of all the Lake Superior missionaries was Father Frederic Baraga. Born in Slovenia (part of present-day Yugoslavia) in 1797, Frederic Baraga was a wealthy and well-educated man. He studied under private tutors at Laibach in present-day Yugoslavia. Then he went to Vienna and attended the Royal Gymnasium and the University of Vienna. He entered the holy order at the Laibach Seminary in 1823. An accomplished linguist, Baraga came to America in 1830.

After five years of working among the Ottawa Indians near the site of present-day Harbor Springs and Grand Rapids, he moved to the Lake Superior area. For nine years he was based in La Pointe on Madeline Island. There he built the Church of St. Joseph and traveled throughout the region by canoe, schooner, dog team and on snowshoes—which is why he became known as the "Snowshoe Priest." His work took him north and west to Grand Portage and Fond du Lac and east to L'Anse.

Father Baraga explained the needs of the Lake Superior Indian missions to his native countrymen so effectively that they sent money and priests to support his work. Father Franz Pierz came to Grand Portage in 1838 and Father Otto Skolla arrived in La Pointe in 1845.

In 1844, Father Baraga moved from La Pointe to L'Anse (now in Michigan) where he had constructed a log chapel (a replica of this chapel is open to the public in Assinins—see entry 77.) There, Father Baraga served the Irish and German Catholic miners who had been attracted to the Keweenaw Peninsula by the copper boom, but his major interest remained the Chippewa Indians. Aside from his pastoral duties, Father Baraga found time to translate the Bible and other religious materials for his Chippewa converts and to prepare a Chippewa grammar book and dictionary.

In 1853, Father Baraga was consecrated as Bishop of Amyzonia and Vicar Apostolic of Michigan and moved to Sault Ste. Marie where his restored home is now open to visitors (see entry 47). In 1857 he became a full bishop and was transferred in 1866 to Marquette. During the 1850s and 60s, he watched the iron and copper country of Michigan's Upper Peninsula develop rapidly. An extremely active traveler, he kept a diary that recounts his work with the fishermen, miners and other settlers in the small towns along the lake shore.

He established schools and churches, found teachers and priests to work in them, and kept the area's Catholic religious and educational complex running smoothly.

Father Baraga died in Marquette in 1868 at the age of 71, and was buried in the crypt of St. Peter's Cathedral (see entry 66). Near L'Anse is the Shrine of the Snowshoe Priest with a commanding 35-foot bronze statue of Father Baraga, looking out over Keweenaw Bay. It stands in memory of his extraordinary accomplishments and his dedication to the people of the region (see entry 71).

There were also other outstanding missionaries who came to Lake Superior. One of them was Protestant minister Sherman Hall of New Hampshire. He was sent to establish a mission at La Pointe and to minister to the Chippewa by the American Board of Commissioners for Foreign Missions in Boston. From 1831 to 1853, Hall directed the La Pointe mission and at least four other smaller missions in the area. He established schools and mission churches and translated various works into the Chippewa language.

Many others also gave their energies to spread the Christian gospel on Lake Superior's frontier. Among the more notable were: James Evans, a Canadian Methodist missionary who served the area briefly before moving north to work with the Indians on Lake Winnipeg; James Peet, a Methodist from western New York, who came to the village of Superior in the 1850s; John H. Pitezel, another Methodist, who ministered to both the Indians and white settlers of Sault Ste. Marie and the Keweenaw Peninsula; and William Thurston Boutwell, who worked at the Indian mission school at Fond du Lac.

The diaries and letters of these Lake Superior missionaries are a rich source of information for those who want more insight into the rigorous and demanding life of the pioneer. These writings, which paint a detailed picture of life in the Lake Superior wilderness and document the changes that took place during the mid-1800s, are described by Grace Lee Nute in her book, *Lake Superior.*

Father Baraga cross, Shroeder, Minn.

77. ASSININS*

[Hy 41, seven miles north of L'Anse]

Assinins was named for Chief Edward Assinins, the first Chippewa Indian to be baptized by Father Frederic Baraga in 1844. This was the last mission Father Baraga established before he was appointed Bishop of Upper Michigan. With funds contributed by European Catholic congregations, Father Baraga founded a school to prepare Indians for employment. Near a replica of his original chapel stands a stone statue of Father Baraga with two Indian parishioners.

North of the chapel lies an old graveyard where Indians, fur traders and pioneer white settlers are buried together. The chapel was once occupied by a Capuchin monastery. It now houses the Keweenaw Bay Tribal Center, the activities of which are considered by some to be an extension of the work started by Father Baraga. The center contains headquarters for the Head Start Program, Indian Health Service, Home School Coordinator, Law Enforcement Program, Keweenaw Bay Tribal Council chambers and the Keweenaw Bay Tribal Construction Company. Among the several buildings here, visitors should be sure to see the handsome old stone house, which served for years as an orphanage. Visitors are welcome and it is well worth stopping by to see the buildings and to visit with the staff there.

78. HOUGHTON AND HANCOCK

[Hy 41]

The opening of Ransom Sheldon's store on the south side of Portage Lake in 1852 marked the beginning of the present city of Houghton. Seven years later Hancock's development began on the opposite side of the lake, with the establishment of a store by Christopher Douglas. As copper mining developed in the area, the towns on opposite sides of Portage Lake grew and became supply centers for the mining industry. Although Hancock was named for the famous John Hancock, signer of the Declaration of Independence, Houghton received its name from the man most responsible for the development of copper mining in Michigan's Upper Peninsula — Douglass Houghton.

Houghton, a graduate of Rensselaer School in Troy, New York, was invited to Michigan in 1830 to deliver a series of lectures on chemistry and geology in Detroit. He stayed on, serving as surgeon and botanist on the Schoolcraft expedition to the source of the Mississippi in 1832.

Twice elected mayor of Detroit, Houghton was appointed state geologist in 1837. He traveled the south shore of Lake Superior five times in the course of his work, and wrote a report in 1841 indicating that copper existed in Michigan's Upper Peninsula. Though the fact was long known, the report sparked a mining boom on the Keweenaw Peninsula.

In 1845 when Houghton was engaged in further mineral surveys for the federal government, his canoe swamped off Eagle River in a heavy snowstorm and he drowned. A marker commemorating Houghton and his contribution to the area can be

Houghton and Portage Lake with early passenger steamer.

found in the Houghton City Park, located in the business district.

The Keweenaw waterway, running between the towns of Houghton and Hancock, takes its name from an Indian word meaning "where a portage is made." This old portage route, used by the voyageurs as well as the Indians, led from Keweenaw Bay through Portage Lake to Lake Superior.

In 1873 the Portage Lake and Lake Superior Ship Canal was completed, financed by a federal land grant. The canal provided a better transportation route for Portage Lake communities, a shortcut across southern Lake Superior for marine traffic and a safe haven from Lake Superior's brutal storms.

The Houghton-Hancock Lift Bridge, spanning the waterway, is the latest in a succession of bridges, the first of which replaced a ferry here in 1876. The present bridge was completed in 1959 at a cost of twelve million dollars. Automobile traffic crosses on the upper level and rail traffic on the lower. The moving portion of the bridge, which raises up to let ships pass beneath, weighs 2,200 tons.

HOUGHTON/HANCOCK SITES OF INTEREST

Michigan Technological University. Through the efforts of legislator Jay Hubbell, the Michigan School of Mines, now called Michigan Technological University, was established in 1885. It was sited on land given by Hubbell to the city of Houghton. On campus, the A.E. Seaman Mineralogical Museum contains a fine collection of Michigan minerals. It is open to the public and free.

Suomi College, Quincy Street. This coeducational Lutheran school offers associate degrees in arts and commerce. Founded in 1896 at Hancock by the Suomi Synod of the Finnish Evangelical Lutheran Church, the school's location reflects the presence of a substantial Finnish population, attracted to the early Keweenaw mining communities. Old Main*, a three-story Richardsonian Romanesque building on Quincy Street, is a good example of Jacobsville sandstone construction (see entry No. 72).

Houghton County Courthouse*, 401 East Houghton Street. This building was constructed in 1887 when mining and prosperity in the area peaked. The architect, J.B. Sweatt of Marquette, modeled it in the Second Empire style and used local building materials--sandstone from a local quarry, brick from Ripley and iron and wood from Marquette. A Calumet artist did the decorative plaster work. County government offices still occupy the building.

Old Houghton Town Hall, now Michigan Technological University.

Quincy Mine Shaft House, Hancock.

Quincy Mine at Hancock is a symbol of the Keweenaw's copper mining country. Although it has been out of operation since 1945, the mine still retains a commanding presence on the bluffs at Hancock.

Opened in 1848, the Quincy Mine was slow to show a profit. By 1860, $900,000 of Eastern capital had been invested and the mine still operated at a loss. But ultimately it became a highly productive mine, repaying investors many times over. These were mainly Massachusetts residents. In fact, the mine was named after Quincy, Massachusetts. The mine earned the nickname "old reliable" after paying dividends for at least 50 years.

In the beginning, miners chiseled copper from cross veins in the rock formations by hand. Later, compressed air drills made the task easier. Much of the copper produced in later years was reclaimed from the stamp sands left over from earlier milling operations (see "Copper Mining," p. 124).

Quincy Mine Hoist, Hy 41. Installed in 1920, this was the largest steam mine hoist in the world. Bruno Nordberg, a Finnish immigrant and engineer, invented the hoist which could lift a ten ton load of copper from a depth of more than 6,000 feet at the rate of 3,200 feet per minute. Today the hoist is housed in a brick, four-story hoist house* which is open daily to the public as a mining museum. ($)

Quincy Hill House, Hy 41, a few blocks from the Quincy Mine Hoist. This house was built in 1871 for the general manager of the Quincy Mine. Restored and open to the public, the home contains 19 rooms. Built almost entirely of white pine, the white frame clapboard structure is Italianate in style. Open summer afternoons, 1-5 p.m. ($)

Quincy Mine Hoist.

79. RIPLEY

[Hy M 26, off Hy 41]

The Arcadian Copper Mine at Ripley provides tours for visitors from June to mid-October. Entrance is through an adit or opening drilled into the side of a hill. ($)

Of the many sites relating to copper mining, the Quincy Mine Hoist and Museum, the A.E. Seaman Mineralogical Museum at Michigan Technological University and the Arcadian Copper Mine at Ripley —taken together—will give the visitor the best overall understanding of copper mining on the Keweenaw Peninsula.

80. HOUGHTON COUNTY HISTORICAL MUSEUM

[On Hy M 26, Lake Linden]

This building, constructed in 1917 as the main mill office of the Calumet and Hecla Mining Company, once housed the offices of the mine manager, foreman and chief chemist. Calumet and Hecla ran stamp mills which crushed and leached out the copper ores, at both Hubbell and Lake Linden, towns located on Torch Lake. These operations became extremely important to the company when, early in the twentieth century, a reclamation plant was built here to refine the copper bearing sands accumulated from earlier stamp milling operations.

The mill office building was donated to the Houghton County Historical Society in 1963 when the corporation consolidated its operations in Calumet.

Houghton County Historical Museum.

The museum now has displays, inside and on the grounds, pertaining to life in the copper country. Among these are scale models of underground mines, relics of the lumber and railroading industries and scenes of early home life. The forestry and mining displays are especially worthwhile. One of the region's first telephone switchboards, which served the C & H Company for many years, was removed for display at the Ford Museum in Dearborn. Open daily and Sunday afternoon, May-September. ($)

South of Lake Linden is a secondary road that runs past the Natural Wall rock ravine. This small ravine has a rock wall that looks as if it were made of cut stone blocks, laid by a stone mason. People at the Houghton County Historical Museum can give detailed directions on how to find it.

81.   BIG TRAVERSE BAY HISTORIC DISTRICT*

This area, lying on the eastern shore of the Keweenaw Peninsula, is readily accessible from Hy 26 at Lake Linden. A mill was built at Big Traverse Bay in 1880 to process logs floated down the Traverse River. Finnish immigrants began a small fishing village here and built homes, saunas and a schoolhouse for their children. At the present time, residents include commercial fishing families and a number of summer residents.

Early day commercial fishing camp.

Former Calumet and Hecla Community Library Building, overseen by statue of Alexander Agassiz.

82. CALUMET

[Hy 41]

Edwin Hulbert, a nephew of Henry Schoolcraft and a civil engineer, discovered and explored the Calumet conglomerate lode from 1856 to 1864. While surveying a road designed to run from Copper Harbor to Ontonagon, he found pieces of surface rock which contained large amounts of copper. This initial find and his further explorations enabled Hulbert to identify and accurately define the Calumet conglomerate lode. He invested in lode land and attempted to turn his discovery into a profitable mining venture.

Lacking the capital to do this, he eventually turned to Quincy A. Shaw of Boston who, in turn, involved Alexander Agassiz, son of naturalist Louis Agassiz. Together they lent funds, managerial skills and technical knowledge to the mining operations.

The details of Hulbert's loss of control over the conglomerate are highly controversial. Whatever the merits of Hulbert's claims, Shaw and Agassiz assumed control. Hulbert, who formed the Calumet Mine in 1861 and opened the Hecla Mine in 1866, failed to make the businesses profitable.

Alexander Agassiz assumed management of the operations in 1867. Four years later, the two companies merged to become the Calumet and Hecla Company (C&H). The Shaw-Agassiz family controlled Calumet-Hecla for four decades and the Bostonians reaped great riches. Hulbert, although by no means a pauper, always considered himself cheated on the business.

Calumet, Red Jacket, Blue Jacket, Yellow Jacket, Laurium, Tamerack, Rambultown, Lake Linden and Hubbell—all these settlements sprang up around the mining operations. Some of the villages owed their unusual names to the American Indians. Red Jacket took its name from a skilled orator of the Seneca Nation who died in 1830. In return for his services as messenger for the British during the American Revolution, he was supposedly rewarded with a bright red jacket. Calumet, which merged with the community of Red Jacket in 1869, was named for the traditional Indian pipe of peace.

By 1869 Calumet had grown into a boom town with citizens of many nationalities all searching for employment in the mines. Between 1870 and 1910 Calumet Township experienced a steady population growth, reaching almost 33,000 people in 1910. During flush times in Calumet, a public library, a 37-room school and at least 20 churches were built on company property and more than 1,000 homes, owned by the company, housed mine employees. Downtown Calumet had the first paved sidewalks in the state. Unlike many short-lived gold and silver mining towns in the West, Calumet and other towns that originated from copper and iron mining in the northern Great Lakes area became permanent communities.

Quincy Mine Shaft No. 2, circa 1908.

Throughout most of its history as a separate company (1871-1967), Calumet and Hecla stayed on top as the largest and most profitable copper mining enterprise in Michigan. Dividends totaled $238 million by 1949.

By the late nineteenth century, however, the productive open pit copper mines of the West made it harder and harder for Michigan's underground copper mines to compete (see "Copper Mining," p.124). From 1917 on, copper production in Michigan steadily declined. Calumet Township's population shrank by half between 1910 and 1930. The Calumet and Hecla Company continued operations until Universal Oil Products, Inc. purchased the property in 1967.

Visitors to Calumet will notice a new mine shaft building at the eastern edge of town, just off Hy 41. In 1973, the Homestake Mining Company, in partnership with International Nickle Company, began exploratory work to study the feasibility of renewing copper mining operations in the area.

Calumet has many nineteenth century buildings which give the town a unique character. Handsome churches and business structures of the last century abound, many constructed of red brick and sandstone. The ethnic background of the community is largely Finnish and Cornish. The legacy of the early miners can be seen in the town's ethnic organizations, festivals, street signs, and family names, and on restaurant menus. The current population numbers a little over 1,000, only three percent of the boom town count.

Slavs march in patriotic parade, Calumet, 1920s.

CALUMET SITES OF INTEREST

Calumet Theatre*, 340 6th Street. Built as an opera house in 1900, the theater seats 1,200 and was an unusually large building for its time. Among the stars who played to audiences here were Sarah Bernhardt, Maude Adams and Lillian Russell. Now used for motion pictures and other kinds of entertainment, the theater has undergone substantial restoration which, when completed, will bring back its turn-of-the-century appearance.

Calumet and Hecla Industrial District*. This area, formerly known as Red Jacket, consists of ten buildings

Calumet Theatre, 1907.

Calumet and Hecla Machine Shop, Calumet.

adjoining the village of Calumet. The Calumet and Hecla Mining Company constructed all of the buildings for their employees and business operations. Red Jacket adjoined the Hecla and Torch Railroad tracks on the west and Calumet Avenue on the east.

Coppertown, U.S.A. Universal Oil Products, Inc. has designed Coppertown, U.S.A. to be an historical,

educational and tourist complex that will reflect the mining history and ethnic heritage of the "copper country." Elaborate plans call for the refurbishment of the Calumet and Hecla Mine headquarters buildings and the addition of a number of new buildings. There will be shops and a restaurant in the converted C&H Roundhouse; a motor hotel; an ethnic center in the C&H Pattern Storage Building, Pattern Shop and

Warehouse; a visitors' center in the Mining Captain's Office; a reconstructed blacksmith shop in the company's old blacksmith shop; and a library museum in the C&H Community Library Building. So far, most of these plans are still on paper.

One building that is ready for visitors is the former C&H Community Library Building, built in 1898, at Red Jacket Road and Mine Street. The building originally contained an employees' library and bathhouse. Built at the suggestion of company president Agassiz in a year when the company paid a very large dividend, the library circulated over 100,000 books. In addition to its regular collection, the library contained 6,000 foreign language books, current periodicals, public documents, maps and a children's section in the basement. A number of volumes from the original collection are on display for visitors.

The building, like the C&H Office, is constructed of grey quartz and of polygon-shaped "poor rock," taken from mine tailings. Some of the building's features include red brick door heads, windows and gable peaks and 46 red sandstone windowsills. The building now houses historic records of the C&H Company, which are used for research purposes, Coppertown U.S.A's administrative offices and materials relating to the boom times in copper mining. Next to the building is a copper statue of a seated Alexander Agassiz in full academic regalia.

83. CENTRAL

[Hy 41]

Immigrants from Cornwall, England first settled Central in 1854. They brought to the mining industry their skill in blasting hard rock with gunpowder to remove the ore. Central Mine employed the Cornishmen, who built at least 130 two-story frame homes in the town. When the ore was exhausted in 1898, the mine closed and most of the workers moved away. Central has today become almost a "ghost" town but summer residents are making plans to restore some of the miners' homes.

CENTRAL SITES OF INTEREST

Central Mine Historic District* is comprised of 18 miners' homes, the restored home of the Central Mine's manager, a church, and scattered ruined and abandoned mine buildings.

Central Mine Yesteryear Museum, 216 Pewabic Street. This museum is housed in an 1860 home. ($)

Central Mine Methodist Episcopal Church* was built in 1869 through the joint efforts of the Cornish miners and the Central Mining Company. Although large congregations attended the church regularly during the mining boom, attendance dwindled after the mine closed. The church closed in 1899 but

Central Mine Church reunion, 1920s.

in 1907 it was decided to hold annual homecoming celebrations there for former Central residents. These homecomings, held on a Sunday in July each year, have become a well-attended tradition.

84. FORT WILKINS STATE PARK

[One mile east of Copper Harbor, (P-H-C-F-B)]

Fort Wilkins* was built in 1844 to protect copper prospectors from potentially hostile Indians and to keep law and order in the mining country. Federal troops manned the fort from 1844-46 and again from 1867-70, after which it was abandoned. The fort then became a popular place for local summer picnics and celebrations. It continued to be used for this purpose until Houghton and Keweenaw Counties purchased the site in 1921. Shortly afterward, it was deeded to the state of Michigan for the establishment of an historic landmark and public park. During the 1930s, federal WPA (Works Progress Administration) workers began restoring the fort, an activity which still continues today.

The Fort Wilkins park exemplifies a mid-nineteenth century frontier military outpost. Fifteen buildings of the fort are as they were at the height of the copper boom. These include the bakehouse, hospital, quartermaster's store, sutler's store, ice house, powder magazine, two company barracks, two mess halls and three officers' quarters.

Within the park, visitors will also find the Pittsburgh and Boston Company's abandoned copper mine shafts; the Copper Harbor Range Light Station;

and the Copper Harbor Lighthouse. The lighthouse, located on Hays Point, was built in 1866 and used until 1919. It was restored in 1933 and again in 1975. The lighthouse, accessible only by boat from Copper Harbor, contains a small marine museum.

Slide shows and programs are held on summer evenings at Fort Wilkins Park. A slide-tape show explaining the history of the fort is offered to visitors in the park entrance building. Open 8 a.m. to 10 p.m. daily in summer. ($)

(Numbered entries continued on p. 129)

Fort Wilkins, a restored century-old frontier military outpost.

COPPER MINING

Hundreds of millions of years ago, a lesion in the earth's crust left rich deposits of copper beneath Michigan's Upper Peninsula. A billion years later an army of Cornishmen, determined to get rich, came to the area with picks and shovels in hand. It was the coming of the Cornishmen in the 1840s that marked the beginning of commercial exploitation of copper deposits in the richest copper-producing area of Lake Superior—the Keweenaw Peninsula of upper Michigan.

Copper has been mined longer than any other metal in the Great Lakes region. For centuries, Indians used copper to make utensils and weapons. The Hopewellian Indians used Lake Superior copper to fashion artifacts, many of which have been found in Hopewell mounds in southern Ohio. Ancient Indian copper workings on Isle Royale near Thunder Bay are still visible (see entry 23).

French traders reported finding copper in the Lake Superior area in the seventeenth century. The first European to engage in copper mining operations on Lake Superior was probably Louis Denis, Sieur de la Ronde. In the late 1730s he established a short-lived copper mining operation, probably near the mouth of the Iron River in Michigan's Upper Peninsula. In 1772, Alexander Henry and his associates—Englishmen operating under the authority of a royal charter—prospected for copper, first on the Ontonagon River near Victoria, Michigan (see entry 93) then on the northeastern coast of the lake between Point Mamainse and the Montreal River. Both ventures quickly failed.

While many people knew that copper was present in the Lake Superior area, it was not until 1841 that two events stimulated concerted mining efforts. First, Douglass Houghton, Michigan's first state geologist, published an official report concerning the wealth of copper around the lake. Then a Detroit businessman, Julius Eldred, started a well-publicized campaign to remove a large copper boulder from Ontonagon and put it on public display in Detroit.

The Ontonagon boulder, still located on Indian land not ceded to the U.S. government, belonged to the Chippewa Indians. Eldred paid an Indian chieftain a small sum for it, but failed on his first try to move the 6,000-pound rock. The next summer he succeeded, using tracks and a small railroad car, only to have the boulder seized by the U.S. govern-

Ancient mining on Lake Superior.

ment. Eldred was compensated and the boulder taken to Washington, D.C. for display at the Smithsonian Institution.

The copper rush began in 1843 and reached a climax three years later. Prospectors began digging in the Copper Harbor and Ontonagon River areas, armed mainly with picks, dynamite and camping gear. Many were Wisconsin lead mining veterans.

The federal government, faced with the problem of developing a mineral land policy for the copper country, first chose to apply a leasing policy set forth in an 1807 law. The War Department stationed an agent at Copper Harbor to issue permits to prospectors in 1843. Once a prospector located copper, he could apply for a lease with the right to explore for a year and to mine for three. He had the option to renew the three-year mining privilege twice. In return for the right to mine, the lessee agreed to pay the U.S. government six percent of the value of minerals taken in the first three years and ten percent thereafter.

The government abandoned the leasing policy in 1846 because it was so difficult to administer. In 1847 it called for an identification of Lake Superior mineral lands. Once identified, these lands were to be sold at a minimum price of five dollars per acre. The minimum was reduced three years later to $1.25 per acre, the same price that applied to other kinds of land in the public domain. Meanwhile the lands had to be surveyed. Douglass Houghton had contracted with the U.S. government to do a combined topographical and geological survey in 1844. He was engaged in this work when he drowned near Eagle River in the fall of 1845 (see entry 89).

It quickly became apparent that mining Keweenaw copper would require considerable capital. Small sums of money were enough to exploit the mass copper near the surface, but the tunneling and handling of amygdaloid and conglomerate ores required substantial investments. (Amygdaloid ore contains pure copper in almond-shaped cavities and conglomerate is a rock formation with copper widely dispersed.) Eventually, these more complex ores produced greater quantities of copper than the mass copper deposits.

Mining companies with substantial capital, often from Boston, formed in the mid-1840s to exploit the various types of ores found in the Copper Harbor, Ontonagon River and Portage Lake regions. One of the most successful early mining operations was the Pittsburgh and Boston Company, which opened the Cliff Mine in the Copper Harbor area, a lode rich in mass copper. Before its demise in 1870, the Cliff Mine paid its stockholders more than $2.5 million in profits, an estimated 2,000 percent return on their original investments.

The early and very successful mass copper mines in the Ontonagon area were the Minesota (that was the way they spelled it) Mine and the National Mine. A mine destined to become world famous, the Quincy Mine at Houghton opened in 1848; the Pewabic opened in the same area in 1856; and the Franklin Mine near Portage Lake was opened by the Civil War. The Calumet and Hecla Mine at Calumet was in production in 1866. By 1860, 33 companies were mining the copper riches of the Keweenaw, with a total investment of more than $4 million.

Following a brief depression in copper mining after the Civil War, production increased. Approximately 25 million pounds of copper were produced in 1872. Michigan's annual copper production rose gradually to 233 million pounds in 1908 and reached an all-time high of almost 266 million pounds during World War I.

Despite this production record, Michigan shaft copper mining felt the edge of western competition in the late nineteenth century, and Michigan's production accounted for less and less of the national output. Michigan's production, which amounted to 80 percent of the national output from 1845-75, slipped to 37 percent from 1876-1900. In the following years, Michigan's production decreased steadily, accounting for 16.5 percent of the total national copper production from 1901 to 1925, 5.2 percent in 1960 and 3.9 percent in 1970.

In spite of western competition, the Michigan mines continued to produce well and earn large profits for their stockholders. The Quincy Mine won the nickname "Old Reliable" because of its consistently good earning record in the late nineteenth and early twentieth centuries. The Calumet and Hecla Mine returned great profits to the Boston investors who owned it, paying a stock dividend of 700 percent as late as 1923. Profits of Michigan copper companies ranged between 16 and 31 percent during World War I.

However, as copper mining in Michigan became less competitive with open pit operations in Montana and Arizona, one company after another suspended operations. The Quincy Mine closed in 1931 after 83 years of continuous production. It opened again and produced from 1937 to 1945 operating more than 6,000 feet below the surface. Calumet and Hecla ceased all mining operations at Calumet in the 1960s. Recently subsidiaries of the

Cliff Mine, 1850s.

Homestake Mining Company and the International Nickel Company began exploratory, developmental mining at Calumet. But in the spring of 1978, Homestake cut its staff to one person—a caretaker. The going price for copper did not justify mining operations.

Today, the White Pine Mine produces Michigan's entire copper output and 70 percent of the copper generated in the Lake Superior region (see entry 95). Large capital investments have permitted highly automated underground mining and a smelting facility adjacent to the mine.

It was recently estimated that only one percent of the Keweenaw's copper resources have been mined. Under the right market conditions, the peninsula could conceivably become a major copper producing area again. Nevertheless, the area gives the visitor the impression of a mining region whose glory has passed. It is an area of abandoned mines; old mining towns—some almost vacant and some flourishing; immense natural beauty; and many ethnic reminders of those immigrants from Cornwall, Finland, Germany, Ireland, Sweden and Italy who once manned the copper mines.

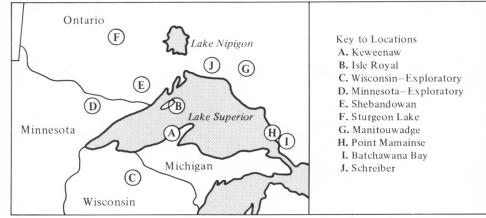

Key to Locations
A. Keweenaw
B. Isle Royal
C. Wisconsin—Exploratory
D. Minnesota—Exploratory
E. Shebandowan
F. Sturgeon Lake
G. Manitouwadge
H. Point Mamainse
I. Batchawana Bay
J. Schreiber

COPPER ORE DISTRICTS OF LAKE SUPERIOR

The Keweenaw is not the only Lake Superior area that has been mined for copper. Commercial copper mining on Isle Royale in Lake Superior continued from 1845 to 1899. Currently more than 40 firms, both Canadian and American, remain interested in the copper potential of northern Wisconsin and some are prospecting. Copper-nickel resources in Minnesota's Superior National Forest are also under exploration.

On the Canadian side of the lake, mid-19th century prospectors sought copper as eagerly as did the miners who poured into the Keweenaw in the 1840s. Many small discoveries and small mining operations dotted the Ontario side of the lake shore. But expectations were never quite fulfilled. Today Shebandowan, Sturgeon Lake, Manitouwadge, Point Mamainse, Batchawana Bay and Schreiber all have operable nonferrous mines that produce copper, as well as some zinc, lead, silver and in one case, nickel.

Miners pause for a portrait after a day's work in the Calumet and Hecla Mine, circa 1907.

This beach between Copper Harbor and Eagle River is typical of many isolated spots on Lake Superior.

85. COPPER HARBOR

[Hy 26]

In 1843, the U.S. government established a land office on Porter's Island, just offshore from Copper Harbor, in an effort to regularize miners' claims. Prospectors rapidly descended upon the Copper Harbor area, following the discovery of copper there in 1843. The rush reached its peak in 1846 and turned Copper Harbor into a boom town. Details about the town's early history are given on a sign in downtown Copper Harbor, erected by the Keweenaw County Road Commission.

Also in the area are the Estivant Pines. This stand of virgin white pine includes trees up to 20 feet in circumference and over 100 feet in height. Backpacking trails from here lead to Lac LaBelle and Bete Grise. At the latter site stands one of three lighthouses located on the tip of the Keweenaw Peninsula. The other two are at Copper Harbor and Eagle Harbor.

86. LAKE SUPERIOR DRIVE

[Hy 26 from Copper Harbor to Eagle River]

An unusually beautiful drive, largely along the Lake Superior shore, offers the traveler a view of sand and pebble beaches, sand dunes, the surf dashing against the rocky shoreline, waterfalls and the north woods. There are many turnoffs and pleasant roadside rest stops for picnickers.

87.   BROCKWAY MOUNTAIN SCENIC DRIVE

Brockway Mountain Scenic Drive is a high road stretching from Copper Harbor to Eagle River. It provides as fine a view of Lake Superior and passing ships as you can find on the Keweenaw. Daniel "Dad" Brockway, for whom the drive is named, came to the Upper Peninsula as government blacksmith on the L'Anse Indian reservation in the early 1840s. Later he became the agent for the Cliff Copper Mine.

88.   EAGLE HARBOR

[Hy 26]

Holy Redeemer Church*.   The first priest to be ordained in the Diocese of Marquette by Bishop Baraga built this church in 1854. The white pine pulpit is unique because of the confessional housed beneath it.   White pine was also used for the tabernacle and baptismal font.   Another church worth viewing in Eagle Harbor is the Episcopal Church, a contemporary of the Holy Redeemer.

Eagle Harbor Schoolhouse* was built in 1853 and restored in the 1920s as a national shrine for members of the Knights of Pythias, a fraternal organization.   One of the early teachers, Justus Rathbone, directed a dramatic production called "Damon and Pythias" there.   Later, in 1864 in Washington, D.C. he wrote the ritual for the new Knights of Pythias.

The U.S. Coast Guard Lighthouse, a red brick structure, was built in 1871. Visitors may stroll around the grounds.

Eagle Harbor Lighthouse.

89. EAGLE RIVER

[Hy 26]

The Cliff, the first mass copper mine to be worked on the peninsula, is located here. Between 1846 and 1870, it produced 38 million pounds of copper. Just offshore, Douglass Houghton, Michigan state geologist, drowned in 1845. A memorial to Houghton stands along Hy 26 at the southern edge of town. A Keweenaw County Road Commission sign stands just across the road, giving details of the early history of Eagle River. The Keweenaw County Courthouse, a two-story wooden structure with some Greek Revival architectural touches is also worth seeing.

90.   TWIN LAKES STATE PARK

[Hy 26, (P-H-C-F-B-S)]

This beautifully wooded park, right along the roadside, has drinking water and toilet facilities.

91. ONTONAGON

[Hy 45]

Because of the natural harbor here, Ontonagon became a lumber shipping port and in 1852, the Ontonagon Lighthouse* was built. The present lighthouse replaced the original in 1866 and was moved to the end of the west pier in 1884. The light tower stands three stories high and the one-and-a-half story dwelling contains nine rooms. With the decline in Great Lakes shipping, the lighthouse stopped service in 1964. It now stands back from the river and serves as a station for the Coast Guard Auxiliary. The lighthouse was presented to the Ontonagon County Historical Society, which hopes to restore it.

Ontonagon County Historical Museum, River Street. The museum contains mining and logging exhibits, local photographs, and artifacts of pioneer living. Open Monday through Saturday, Memorial Day through Labor Day.

92.   ROCKLAND

[Hy 45]

Rockland originated as a mining boom town in the 1850s. It was famous for mass copper and for the riotous behavior of its Irish and Cornish miners. Many of the mining operations were financially unsuccessful. Among the more prosperous, however, was the Minnesota Copper Mine, which operated between 1847 and 1865. A marker there tells its history. Visitors will find much evidence of nineteenth century mining operations in the area and may wish to stop and explore the abandoned diggings.

93.   VICTORIA

[Off Hy 45 southwest of Rockland]

Victoria is silent, a ghost town now as it has been for half a century since the Victoria Mine closed shortly after World War I. When the mine was in operation, the town's population swelled to 1,800–among them many immigrant mine workers.

Victoria, once a bustling mining community, is now a ghost town.

The Society for the Restoration of Old Victoria, formed in 1973, is in the process of restoring a number of old miners' cabins dating from the mid-nineteenth century. Two log structures, the Arvola home and one other dwelling, have so far been restored. These are open daily in summer. ($)

A marker at Victoria recounts the exploits of Alexander Henry and his associates. Interested in discovering and mining copper on the shores of Lake Superior, they began copper mining in 1771-72 under royal charter from the King of England. It was a short-lived venture which angered the fur traders, who feared that the miners would spoil their happy relationship with the Indians.

Visitors to the area may also visit the remains of the mine buildings nearby and the Victoria Dam, a source of hydropower for the Upper Peninsula Power Company, just down the road.

94. OTTAWA NATIONAL FOREST

(P-H-C-F-B-S)

Established in 1931, this national forest covers 886,000 acres. Headquarters are at Ironwood, Michigan. The Sylvania Recreation Area is a wilderness area within the forest, where camping, fishing, boating and hiking opportunities abound. Nature programs are held at the Visitor's Center in Watersmeet, where maps and brochures about the national forest are also available.

95. WHITE PINE

[Hy 64]

The White Pine Copper Mine, located here, is the largest copper mining operation left in Michigan. The mine accounts for more than 70 percent of the Lake Superior region's copper ore production. Its underground operations are highly automated and it has onsite smelting facilities. While there are no public tours, visitors can drive by and see it.

96. PORCUPINE MOUNTAINS
   WILDERNESS STATE PARK

[17 miles west of Ontonagon, Hy 107, (P-H-C-F)]

These 58,000 acres of wilderness were established as a park in 1945. One of the few remaining wilderness areas in the Midwest, the park contains the highest mountain range in the Midwest, several miles of rugged Lake Superior shoreline and virgin forests of pine and hardwood. Over 80 miles of hiking trails lead the hiker past secluded lakes and through miles of virgin timber. The trails vary in length, but the ambitious hiker can take advantage of the trailside cabins found in the park, where visitors can stay up to three days. Evidence of past mining operations can be found in the park.

Backpacking in Porcupine Mountains State Park.

97. LAKE SUPERIOR VISTAS

Lying to the west of Porcupine Mountains State Park are three locations that offer fine vistas of Lake Superior. These lie at the western border of the park where the Presque Isle River flows into the lake; at the Black River campground at the mouth of the river (accessible from a secondary road off Hy 2); and at Little Girl's Point (accessible from a secondary road off Hy 2).

Lake Superior vista at McLain Park near Hancock.

Hurley, Wisconsin, 1886.

98. IRONWOOD, MICHIGAN AND HURLEY, WISCONSIN

[Hy 2]

Ironwood is the "mother city" of the surrounding mining area. Lumbering and iron mining fostered its development as well as that of Hurley, just across the Wisconsin border. Ironwood quietly grew as the business and commercial center of the twin towns while Hurley gained a reputation as the most notorious "sin city" of the upper lakes country. "The hell hole of the range," it was famous for gambling, drinking, prostitution and crime and was immortalized by Edna Ferber's book, *Come and Get It*.

Attracted by J. L. Norrie's report in 1884 that he had found iron ore near Ironwood, miners and mine developers from the Marquette and Menominee ranges flocked into the area. A railroad, built from Watersmeet to Ashland in 1885, made the Gogebic range accessible and

mining began the same year. Platted in 1885, Ironwood incorporated as a village in 1887 and received a city charter in 1889, with a population of 7,000. Today 8,700 people live in Ironwood, which was named for one of the early mining captains, John R. Wood, who was nicknamed "Iron."

During the first half-century of development, the Ironwood mines produced more than 100 million tons of high-grade ore. Deep shaft mining and underground tunneling characterized these mines whose ores were found in a steeply-tilted sedimentary belt. The last operable mine in the Gogebic range was the Peterson Mine, located east of Ironwood. It closed early in 1966. A renewal of mining here depends upon the adaptation of the beneficiation processes to the kinds of ores found in the Gogebic range.

As Ironwood grew, Hurley declined due to the low-grade Wisconsin ores and cutover timberland. The population—once swelled to more than 7,000—has dwindled to about 2,300 today. At both Ironwood and Hurley, the traveler can see evidence of past lumbering and mining activities (see "Iron Mining" p. 96).

The Old Iron County Courthouse* at Hurley, designed by L. H. Ruggles, was built in 1892-93 as a town hall for the former town of Vaughn. Upon creation of Iron County in 1893, it went into immediate service as a courthouse. Today, it houses a museum.

Old Iron County Courthouse, Hurley.

The Montreal River, once a water route for the Indians, forms part of the border between Michigan and Wisconsin.

99. MONTREAL

[Hy 77]

Once a prosperous lumbering and mining community, Montreal is now well-known for its nearby ski slopes–Whitecap, Indianhead, Blackjack and Big Powderhorn Mountains. The Montreal Mine produced over 41 million tons of iron ore before it closed in the 1960s. The neat white uniform houses, built for employees of the Oglebay-Norton Mining Company, now belong mostly to skiing families. The Montreal River Lumber Company was also important to the early economic life of Montreal. The company logged much of the local white pine in the late nineteenth and early twentieth centuries. A historical marker adjacent to city hall commemorates Montreal's mining and lumbering past.

100. CHEQUAMEGON BAY, CHEQUAMEGON POINT AND LONG ISLAND

[Hy 2]

The name Chequamegon resulted from an attempt by early French explorers to spell the Chippewa Indian word "sha-gua-wau-me-kong," which means a "long narrow strip of land running into a body of water." Although today Chequamegon Bay and Chequamegon Point are two separate entities on the map, the name actually refers to both the 60-square-mile area of the bay and the sand spit running into it. Like Minnesota Point at Duluth, Chequamegon Point was formed by the action of waves on both sides of a point of land. A half-mile gap separated Chequamegon Point and Long Island for 40 years until early in 1977 when lower lake levels on Superior closed the gap. The island and the point were also joined between 1925-1937, and undoubtedly, at intervals before that date. Chequamegon Point Lighthouse, which stands at the north tip of Long Island, has been recommended as a sanctuary for common terns and piping plovers.

101. KAKAGON AND BAD RIVER SLOUGHS†

[Between Hy 2 and Chequamegon Point]

Waterfowl, fur-bearing animals and fish flourish in these sloughs, which are noted for their scenic beauty. Wild rice beds, covering about 12 square miles of the sloughs, provide a food source for wildlife and an income source for the Chippewa Indians. The entire marsh area, which encompasses about 2,900 acres, belongs to the Bad River Chippewa band. The Indians harvest about 6,000 pounds of wild rice a year. The sloughs are a paradise for sport fishermen, but fishermen are advised to obtain the services of a Chippewa guide to escort them safely through the intricate maze of waterways.

102. BAD RIVER INDIAN RESERVATION

[Hy 2]

Established by the terms of the Treaty of La Pointe in 1854, this Chippewa reservation originally covered 124,234 acres. It now covers 54,912 acres, of which 8,325 are tribally-owned, 13,110 are government-owned and 33,477 are deeded to individual Indians. Timber, the major natural resource of reservation lands, provides some tribal income. Approximately 700 Indians reside on or adjacent to the reservation, which has one town, Odanah.

The Bad River Reservation has 17 miles of beautiful Lake Superior shoreline within its boundaries. The Bad River, from which the reservation takes its name, frequently overflows its banks. This might seem reason enough to term it a "bad" river but, in fact, the name comes from the French "Rivière Mauvais," their translation of a Chippewa word meaning swamp. In their turn, the British mistranslated the French name and the result today is Bad River.

(Numbered entries continued on p. 143)

---

†Included on the National Registry of Natural Landmarks for its importance as a natural site.

THE LUMBER INDUSTRY

The vast stands of virgin timber ringing the Lake Superior shoreline were the region's major source of wealth until the early 1900s. They proved an even richer resource than iron or copper. The solemn, black-barked white pines stretching along the shoreline of Minnesota from the Pigeon River, south through Wisconsin and Michigan, and for a short distance north into Canada, were the most prized of all timber resources. But the shores of Lake Superior also boasted stands of Norway, red, black and jack pines, hemlock, spruce, maple, red oak, white and yellow birch, balsam fir, poplar, tamarack, cedar, ash, aspen and arbor vitae.

The search for timber had moved westward from the forests of Maine, New York and Pennsylvania into the pinelands of the upper Great Lakes. Lake Superior lumbering enjoyed its most prosperous period from 1880 through 1925, but the region's first large-scale lumbering operations had begun in the 1840s on Michigan's Lower Peninsula. In the 1880s the center of lumbering shifted northward to the ten million acres of woodland on the Upper Peninsula. Here the rivers, emptying into both Lakes Superior and Michigan, provided an excellent means of transporting the logs from forest to mill—a role later taken over by the railroads. Michigan's lumber production on Lake Superior was centered in Marquette, Ontonagon, Baraga and Houghton Counties and reached its peak in 1888. In 1900, Michigan was still the leading lumber-producing state in the Union.

The pineries along Wisconsin's Lake Superior shoreline were first logged commercially in the 1870s. Both Superior and Ashland became major lumbering centers (see entries 1 and 103). A prominent figure in Superior-Duluth's lumbering history was Frederick Weyerhaeuser, a Rock Island, Illinois lumberman who earned the name "Pine Land King of the Northwest." Weyerhaeuser secured vast tracts of pine land in northwestern Wisconsin near the twin ports, and fostered a lumber boom there in the 1880s and 1890s. In 1899, 462 million board feet of lumber were shipped through Duluth, although the lumber volume declined steadily thereafter with only 11.6 million feet shipped in 1924. By 1925, only one lumber mill still operated at Duluth.

After exhausting the resources of the south shore of Lake Superior, lumbermen focused their attention on the abundant pine, spruce, balsam, white cedar, birch and poplar lying north of Duluth along the lake. Logging there reached its peak during the first decade of this century. White and Norway pines were logged first and later pulpwood—balsam, cedar, white spruce and tamarack—was harvested. These woods were used for making boxes and crates, telephone poles, railroad ties, pilings and posts. Because of the gorges and falls along the rivers of Minnesota's north shore, lumbermen had to use railroads to carry their logs down to the lake. There, they marked the logs and tied them together into large rafts which they towed south to the Duluth-Superior mills. These log rafts were a familiar sight on Lake Superior well into the twentieth century. In fact, as recently as 1972, the tug JOHN ROEN III made its last log raft run. It pulled a two mile long necklace of Sitka spruce logs—some 450,000 cubic feet of lumber—from Grand Marais, Minnesota to Ashland, Wisconsin.

The Canadian forests along the Ontario shoreline of Lake Superior escaped the lumbering onslaught largely because the coveted white and Norway pines were scarce there. However, Canadian forests have been an important source of pulpwood for many decades. The Thunder Bay area, where lumbering enterprises sprang up in the late 1800s, is currently Canada's largest pulp and paper producing area (see entry 26). Terrace Bay and Marathon both have pulp mills which welcome visitors (see entries 34 and 36).

The Lake Superior lumbering industry prospered because of rich timber resources, market demands of a developing nation, and cheap natural water transportation. Important to that prosperity too were Eastern capital, leadership, and lumbering techniques. Experienced Eastern lumbermen joined the ranks of local entrepreneurs. They brought with them a corps of skilled timber cruisers, loggers, sawyers, teamsters, and rivermen. Plentiful skilled and unskilled local labor, itinerant day labor from the lower Midwest, and immigrant workers—chiefly from Ireland, Sweden, Finland, Norway, French Canada, Scotland, England, and Germany—combined to perform the day-to-day work in the pineries.

The mackinaw-clad workmen lived in temporary logging camps equipped with cook shanties, bunk houses, barns, granaries and blacksmith and carpenter shops. Camps varied in their conditions and comforts, but in each of them, the hardy lumberjacks relieved their daily labors in the evening after supper with cards, storytelling, singing and smoking. Their real entertainment came at the end of the season when they went to town in search of liquor, gambling and female companionship.

The lumbermen's colorful exploits have been romanticized to such a point that it is easy to forget that most of them were moderate in their habits and interested only in earning

Felling white pine, Wisconsin.

the down payment on a farm. Their expertise at telling tall tales and inventing mythical northwoods creatures inspired many a writer. Paul Bunyan and Babe, his great blue ox, are apparently an early twentieth century invention of "someone in Oregon." But the stories of Hugag, Hodag, Splinter Cat and Side-Hill Dodger are authentic northwoods lore.

One such story concerns the mythical Agropelter, the scourge of loggers from Maine to Oregon. A logger could easily pay with his life for passing a hollow tree in which the Agropelter made his home. Resenting the intrusion, the creature would, according to legend, throw a dead branch at the passerby with lethal accuracy. Only one person survived to tell of his encounter with the Agropelter, according to William T. Cox. Cox, Minnesota's first state forester and Conservation Commissioner, was a collector of northwoods lore. Big Ole Kittleson, it seems, was hit with the Agropelter's skillfully-thrown dead branch while cruising timber in the upper St. Croix area. He lived to tell the story because the limb was so punky. Ole reported that the Agropelter "has a slender, wiry body, the villainous face of an ape and arms like muscular whiplashes, with which it can snap off dead branches and hurl them through the air like shells from a six-inch gun."

As the laborers lived humbly in the lumber camps, many of the industry's owners and operators lived ostentatiously in imposing homes and became influential in politics. But such men as Frederick Weyerhaeuser, who became fabulously rich from his empire in pine, were exceptional. Thousands of small lumber businesses reaped only modest profits and many others failed altogether. It was a naturally hazardous and highly competitive business. Lumbermen learned early the wisdom of controlling all phases of production from forest to mill to market. As a result there was a tendency toward consolidation, with larger and stronger businesses buying and controlling smaller ones. Lumbermen also joined together at times to control production, fix prices, develop standards and grading practices, and secure special privileges from the railroads or build new ones.

Throughout this logging boom, the prevalent attitude was that lumber was needed to supply a rapidly-expanding agricultural and industrial economy. Lumbering made jobs. "Clear the forests and farm the land" had long been the American norm for turning a wilderness into a prospering nation. But this philosophy led to the stripping of millions of acres of forest lands that were better suited to growing trees than growing crops. Such was the land on the shores of Lake Superior. In the wake of the ax and the saw came disastrous fires, often caused by the hot dry summers that turned the brush and debris into dry tinder. Fires along the north shore of Minnesota occurred in 1850, 1878, 1910 and almost yearly from 1913 to 1925. Grace Lee Nute writes in her book, *Lake Superior,* "As late as the middle 1930s the land beside the scenic coast drive [from Duluth-Superior to the Canadian border] was practically a continuous forest of blackened stumps." Only with the end of commercial lumbering, the start of systematic fire watches and improved fire fighting methods did the conflagrations cease.

To what use could these lands, denuded of their virgin forests, be put? Many advocated reforestation but the common answer was the traditional one—farming. The enormous labor involved in clearing away stumps and cultivating the light, sandy soils proved, within a few decades, to be a poor investment. The number of farms in the cutover counties of northern Michigan increased from 1900 to 1935 and then began to decline. For those who tried farming, the harvest all too often was hard work, a short growing season, a poor living standard and failure. Today, much of the cutover land is county, state and national forest. It has gradually returned to its wild state; and second growth, which is quite beautiful, has covered the scars of the big cut. In many areas, birches and hardwoods nurture a new stand of majestic white pines.

Cutover land in northern Wisconsin, 1930s.

Bird's eye view of early-day Ashland.

103.   ASHLAND

[Hys 2 and 13]

According to the 1881 *History of Northern Wisconsin*, Ashland was selected as a town site on July 5, 1854 when Asaph Whittlesey and George Kilborn rowed from La Pointe and landed there. The name Ashland was the idea of Martin Beaser, the town's second postmaster. A great admirer of Henry Clay, Beaser wanted to honor him by using Ashland, the name of Clay's Kentucky home.

The financial panic of 1857 prevented the community from becoming well-established, but the selection of Ashland as the Chequamegon Bay terminus for the Wisconsin Central Railroad gave impetus to its later growth. During the early 1870s, Ashland became headquarters for Wisconsin Central Railroad construction gangs. In the summer of 1877 regular train service linked Ashland with Lake Michigan harbors to the southeast.

The combination of railroad facilities and a fine natural harbor—used as a shipping center for both lumber and ore--stimulated the economy. By 1889 four railroads entered Ashland and four ore docks accommodated ships loading ore from the Gogebic range. Three of the docks have since burned and only one remains today, largely unused.

Lumbering, although once a major source of income, did not last forever and the town which had once been on the edge of a dense pine forest found itself sitting amidst cutover land. The University of Wisconsin College of Agriculture then started an experimental farm at Ashland Junction to give would-be farmers advice on how to raise crops on the cutover lands. But the land proved unsuitable for agriculture and today many acres of cutover land have been reforested and wood products once again are a major source of Ashland's income.

104. RADISSON-GROSEILLIERS LANDING SITE

[Hys 2 and 13, on the west side of Ashland]

An historic marker, prepared and erected by the State Historical Society of Wisconsin, commem-orates the landing of Radisson and Groseilliers "at the end of this bay" in 1659. Their trip from Trois Rivières westward into the lake country had great significance in the struggle between England and France to control the fur trade and the continent, because it led directly to the founding of the Hudson's Bay Company. A simple log structure represents the crude fort the two explorers erected for themselves in 1659 — boughs of trees "layed acrosse, one uppon an other."

105. BARKSDALE

[Hy 13]

The DuPont Corporation manufactured explosives that were needed both at copper and iron mines

Ashland lumber mill, circa 1900.

in the area and to clear land for settlement. To be closer to their potential customers, DuPont established a plant here in 1905, naming it for Hamilton Barksdale, a DuPont executive who was made manager of the works. A village for workers sprang up around the plant and homes for company officials lined East Third Street.

By 1913, World War I had created an even more pressing demand for explosives. Between 1913 and 1918, the Barksdale Works of the DuPont Corporation produced more dynamite than any other plant in the world. An additional facility was built in 1950 to produce explosives used in mining taconite, but by 1971 the entire Barksdale operation had been closed down. Area residents hope that the industrial site will be purchased by another corporation.

106. WASHBURN

[Hy 13]

Named for Wisconsin Governor Cadwallader C. Washburn, the town of Washburn sits on a slope facing Chequamegon Bay. It thrived as a sawmill and shipping center from its founding in 1884 until the lumber traffic began to decline. With the creation of Barksdale, a few miles to the south, Washburn enjoyed a business revival as a shopping center for the workers at the explosives plant.

Although Bayfield had been designated the county seat for Bayfield County in 1869, that honor was transferred to Washburn in the election year of 1892 after the issue of location had been voted upon. Bayfield partisans alleged that Washburn supporters won by underhanded electioneering. A small wooden building was hastily erected as a temporary courthouse but in 1894, the permanent Bayfield County Courthouse* was completed at 117 East Fifth Street. The handsome Lake Superior brownstone structure, with a domed cupola, was designed by the Minneapolis firm of Off & Joralemann. The Neo-Classical Revival building has a handsome exterior and the interior woodwork is still in excellent condition.

107. CHEQUAMEGON NATIONAL FOREST

(P-H-C-F-B-S)

The 838,000-acre Chequamegon National Forest takes its name from Chequamegon Bay on Lake Superior. It is divided into three sections, the northernmost of which is in Bayfield County. A U.S. Forest Service district ranger is stationed at Washburn. The forest is rich in lakes and rivers. Many sites, including three ski areas, have been set aside as recreation areas in the forest. The ranger station at Washburn can provide directions to them.

108. BAYFIELD

[Hy 13]

By its name, the city of Bayfield honors British Navy Admiralty Surveyor Henry Bayfield, who prepared charts of Chéquamegon Bay from 1823-1825. Lt. Bayfield's maps of the Great Lakes were

A summer's outing on the steamer, BARKER, at Bayfield.

so accurate that many years later, they vere important in the establishment of commercial shipping lanes and were still consulted well into the twentieth century.

Bayfield had its start in 1856 when a member of the Minnesota territorial legislature, Henry Rice, began the Bayfield Land Company there. The company sold land in anticipation of a railroad link from St. Paul. Visions of a settlement that would rival Chicago in commerce and grain shipping quickly attracted land buyers to the area, but it was some time before the Chicago, St. Paul, Minnesota & Omaha Railroad was actually completed. In the meantime, lumbering and fishing were important activities.

Bayfield had been a fishing port for herring, whitefish and trout in the days of the American Fur Company. With the coming of the railroad, fish became an important commercial item and over six tons a day were shipped to larger cities. By the 1890s Booth Fisheries had at least 500 year-round employees.

Another valuable area resource was Lake Superior brown sandstone, originally quarried on Basswood Island near Bayfield. Once the sandstone's value as a building stone became established, other quarries were started. Lake Superior sandstone was used to construct homes and buildings in many American cities — including Chicago and Brooklyn, where many fine old brownstone row houses have been restored. Bayfield's nineteenth century prosperity is evident today in the lovely Queen Anne and Italianate style homes still standing.

In the 1890s Bayfield became a popular tourist site with flocks of visitors arriving by train or excursion steamer. The railroad built the Island View Hotel in Bayfield for the travelers' comfort, but fire destroyed it in 1913. Nevertheless, tourists continued to come via the six passenger trains arriving daily until the 1920s, when the automobile began to take over.

Frank Boutin's Home* at 7 Rice Avenue was built in 1908 by the son of a pioneer Bayfield resident who became successful in the lumbering and fishing industries. Tours by owner May 1-November 1. ($)

Ravine Nature Trail, beginning at Washington Avenue and Broad Street, leads up the ravine and under an old iron bridge. In the ravine are the remains of old hollowed-out logs that the Bayfield Hydraulic Company used to supply water to Bayfield at the turn of the century. A cement dam was built here across Larsen Creek to prevent a repeat of the 1942 flood that damaged several structures in downtown Bayfield. Overhead is the Rice Avenue iron bridge, built in 1912 to replace an old wooden bridge that had collapsed into the ravine the year before. The 230-foot long bridge is now closed to vehicular traffic but pedestrians can enjoy a view across Chequamegon Bay to Ashland on a clear day. The bridge has been suggested as an

addition to the National Register of Historic Places but has not yet been approved.

Bayfield County Courthouse*. Built in 1883, the courthouse still stands on Washington Avenue between 4th and 5th Streets. A Madison architect, John Nader, designed the Neo-Classical Revival

Bayfield County Courthouse.

The Madeline Island Ferry returns summer visitors to Bayfield harbor.

two-story building of brown Lake Superior sandstone. After the county seat moved to Washburn in 1892, the building was adapted for use as a school gym and a storage place for county records. It housed prisoners of war during World War II. The Bayfield County Historical Society is renovating the handsome building, which has become headquarters and visitor information center for the Apostle Islands National Lakeshore. The headquarters building was formerly located at Little Sand Bay.

Apostle Islands Boat Tours/Ferry to Madeline Island. Excursion boats leave the Bayfield town dock for trips around the Apostle Islands throughout the summer. Visitors may take tours, ranging from two to six hours in duration. ($) The Madeline Island ferry also leaves from this area, making several round trip excursions daily when the lake is ice-free.

LAKE SUPERIOR FISHERIES

Lake Superior whitefish is "in the universal estimation the finest fish that swims. The meat is as white as the breast of a partridge; and the bones are less numerous and larger than in our shad. I never tasted any thing of the fish kind . . . to equal it." So wrote a member of the 1820 expedition that journeyed from Detroit to the sources of the Mississippi River. This eulogy to the fish expressed the sentiments of scores of Indian people, explorers, fur traders, and missionaries who had come to Lake Superior before this expedition, and many area residents and visitors since.

Whitefish formed an important part of the diet of Lake Superior's Indian people. Their villages grew up at points along the lakeshore where fishing was unusually good. Especially famous for whitefish were the rapids of the St. Mary's River. Henry Schoolcraft noted in 1820 that the abundant whitefish sustained 40 lodges of Chippewa there. At the foot of the rapids whitefish "often crowded together in the water in great numbers." In the autumn, skilled Indian fishermen stood upright in swaying canoes. Equipped with long poles and scoop nets, they could take 500 fish in two hours. Dried and smoked, the fish were "a large portion" of the Chippewa winter diet.

Until the early 1800s, Lake Superior's fish supplied food only for local consumption or for expeditions into the interior. The fur trading companies, particularly the Hudson's Bay Company and the American Fur Company, launched Lake Superior's first large-scale commercial fishing businesses. Before 1850 the Hudson's Bay Company maintained fisheries at Fort William and Michipicoten. Part of the catch went to the Detroit market, but much of it went to employees in the company's far-flung operations.

The American Fur Company also developed an extensive commercial fishery as an adjunct to its fur trade on Lake Superior from 1834 to 1841. After conducting a search for the best fishery sites, the company selected Grand Portage, Isle Royale, and La Pointe on Madeline Island as major fishing stations. Minor ones included an island near present-day Duluth, the Montreal River, the Keweenaw Peninsula, Grand Island, Whitefish Point, and Sault Ste. Marie.

At the fishing stations, company employees fished, made barrels and gill nets, and cleaned, salted, and packed the catch—mainly, whitefish, trout, siscowet and herring. Barrels of salted fish went to the Detroit market aboard the company's fleet of boats. A thousand barrels of fish were shipped to Detroit in 1836, and the amount rose steadily until 1839 when nearly 5,000 barrels or one million pounds of fish were shipped.

The depression of the late 1830s, however, brought a swift end to the American Fur Company's commercial fishing business. The Company tried in vain to broaden its markets to New York, the Middle West, and the Mississippi Valley as far south as New Orleans. But commercial fishing ended in 1841 and the company failed the following year. Three rival firms tried to make a go of the fishing business on Lake Superior in the late 1830s, but also gave up in the face of the depressed economy.

Commercial fishing revived on Lake Superior in the 1850s and grew in importance during the balance of the century, producing food for the influx of settlers in mining and lumbering centers. In time, more and more of the catch went to southern lake ports like Milwaukee, Chicago, Cleveland and Detroit for sale and distribution elsewhere.

The 1870 catch amounted to an estimated four million pounds; the 1890 catch was about six million pounds. Important centers were the Bayfield-Ashland-Apostle Islands area; the Keweenaw Peninsula from Ontonagon to L'Anse; Marquette; Whitefish Point; and Sault Ste. Marie. On the Canadian side commercial fishing in the late nineteenth century was centered at Port Arthur (now Thunder Bay), Rossport, and the Slate Islands.

In the late 1880s and 1890s, many American fishermen transferred their gear from the American to the Canadian side of the lake. So pronounced was the exodus that the U.S. Commissioner of Fish and Fisheries reported some former American fishing stations had been virtually abandoned. Fishermen sought the best fishing grounds with little regard for international boundaries.

The commercial exploitation of Lake Superior fish accelerated in the twentieth century, reaching a high point with a 25,500,000 pound harvest in 1941. Since then, the catch level has declined to about eight million pounds a year, partly due to the effects of the invasion of the predatory sea lamprey in the late 1950s.

The composition of the Lake Superior catch has changed greatly over the fishery's 125-year history. Until 1890, whitefish were the prime target, but yields declined sharply during the next 30 years. As whitefish declined, lake trout gained in importance. However, the lake trout catch was eclipsed by the herring catch in 1908. Once scorned as too cheap and undesirable to bother with, herring reached an all-time high yield of about 19

"Trolling," by Currier and Ives, 1888.

million pounds in 1941. Meanwhile, the lake trout fishery averaged only slightly less than five million pounds annually until 1955 when it collapsed due to the sea lamprey.

Chubs have also been important in the Lake Superior fishery. Around the turn of the century, the larger chub species were fished so vigorously that they became commercially extinct by 1907. However, between 1955 and 1965, commercial fishermen were again harvesting chubs—this time, the smaller species. Sturgeon, walleye and smelt have been of minor importance to Lake Superior's commercial fishery over the years. Today, whitefish is the leading commercial species in poundage and economic value.

Fishing methods have also changed greatly over the history of the fishery. In 1850 the small, sturdy mackinaw boats and canoes, and a wide assortment of small boats with oars and sails served as fishing craft. In the 1870s and 1880s, schooners and gill net steamers came into use in the Keweenaw and Marquette fisheries. Then about 1900, gasoline-powered internal combustion engines were introduced, followed by the diesel-powered motors of today.

Methods of catching fish also changed, becoming ever more complex and efficient. The Indian people of Lake Superior used simple bone hooks, spears, weirs, seins, and dip nets. The white fishermen introduced a variety of high-yielding nets. For example, the American Fur Company used gill nets in its fishing business in the 1830s. Gill nets, which hang like anchored curtains in the water and entangle the fish as they try to swim through, came into general use on Lake Superior in the nineteenth century and are still widely-used. Other types are pound nets, fyke nets and trap nets.

Along with better nets came improvements as far as hauling fish-laden nets out of the water. In the 1890s, steam-powered drums were used to retrieve gill nets. At the turn of the century, gasoline engines were harnessed to operate net lifters; later, diesel-powered engines performed the task.

Technological improvements in boats and gear made greater catches possible. Fishermen moved farther and farther from their home ports and fished at greater depths. The vigorous pursuit of Lake Superior fish was not unlike the zeal of the fur traders, lumbermen and miners in exploiting the natural wealth along the shores of Lake Superior.

Concern about the effects of this unbridled harvest emerged as early as the 1880s when fishermen at Chequamegon Bay, Ontonagon and the Keweenaw Peninsula voiced fears that the fisheries would be depleted. Chequamegon Bay was closed to fishing in the late 1880s, reopened in 1891 due to political pressures, and closed again in 1896. Fishermen blamed declining catches on log drives on the rivers and lumber mill refuse, dumped into streams and lakes—practices that fouled the water and spawning grounds. They also blamed increased navigation and overfishing.

In the twentieth century pollutants from industrial plants at some locations also spoiled the fish habitat.

Worst of all for Lake Superior's fish population was the invasion of the sea lamprey. With its suction-like mouth, the lamprey attaches itself to its prey and feeds on its victim's life juices. This eel-like saltwater fish came into the upper Great Lakes from the Atlantic Ocean and Lake Ontario via the Welland and perhaps the Erie canals. Destroying the fisheries of Lakes Huron and Michigan on its way, the voracious predator eventually reached Lake Superior in 1946. By 1951 lake trout, a favored prey of the sea lamprey, began a steep decline. Lake trout catches fell from about five million pounds in 1950 to 380,000 pounds 11 years later.

Scientists fought the intruders by erecting electromechanical barriers on about 100 of Lake Superior's lamprey spawning streams. In 1958, chemists introduced a poison, TFM, which killed lamprey larvae in infested streams. The barriers, coupled with the new lampricide, proved effective and by 1962, sea lamprey populations were down 82 percent.

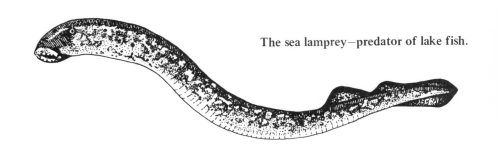

The sea lamprey—predator of lake fish.

Fishing fleet at Bayfield, Wis., wharf.

Long before the sea lamprey invasion, many people recognized the need for government policies to sustain Lake Superior's fish population. For years, fishermen argued that restocking programs would be sufficient, and some of the state governments began restocking lake fish well before 1900. More recently, Ontario, Minnesota, Wisconsin and Michigan began vigorous restocking programs in the wake of the sea lamprey. Lake, rainbow and brown trout as well as coho and chinook salmon are the major fish being introduced—so far, with great success.

Other historic policy initiatives included strict regulation of net size and depth, and rules designed to protect fish during spawning seasons. Since 1875, state officials, charged with responsibility for Great Lakes fisheries, have called for cooperation between the states on these matters and for the establishment of uniform regulatory laws.

In 1907-08, the United States and Canada agreed to joint regulation of Great Lakes fishing. But effective international cooperation did not really begin until 1955 when the two countries joined in a concerted effort to control sea lamprey populations.

Wisconsin now regulates its Lake Superior fishery by limiting to 21 the number of commercial licenses issued. The state's Department of Natural Resources has also set limits on the kind, size and amount of gear, imposed rules to protect spawning fish and closed certain areas to fishing altogether. A Commercial Fisheries Board for Lake Superior, made up of fishermen, processors and public members, determines how catch quotas will be allocated and helps set fishery policy.

Aside from commercial fishing, sport fishing has always been popular on Lake Superior. The lake attracted many fishermen in the mid-1920s when "Uncle Billy" Brown—a skilled fisherman from the West Coast—introduced trolling for trout at Minising, Michigan. Charter boat businesses boomed. By 1950, there were an estimated 47 part-time and 10 full-time charter boat operations on the lake. Today, charter boat businesses are still important and sport fishing for trout and salmon is more popular than ever.

What does the future hold for Lake Superior's commercial and sport fishing industries? It is hard to predict, but it seems certain that much will depend on continued control of the sea lamprey. Also critical will be studies of the relationships between newly-introduced species and native lake fish; continued government efforts to develop uniform fishery policies; and perhaps most important, continued efforts to minimize the industrial and agricultural pollution of Lake Superior.

109. APOSTLE ISLANDS NATIONAL LAKESHORE

(P-H-C-F-B-S)

A survey of the Apostle Islands was undertaken in 1929. It was hoped it would result in the purchase of the islands by the federal government. The

Apostle Islands shoreline encrusted with winter ice.

final survey report, however, did not favor this move–largely because Isle Royale was then being acquired as a national park. By 1970, there had been so many requests to make the Apostle Islands a national park that the Apostle Islands National Lakeshore was officially established. The National Lakeshore will eventually cover 39,000 acres, including 11 miles of shoreline, and will include 20 of the 22 Apostle Islands.

It is not known whether the Apostle Islands were originally named by a Jesuit missionary or by Jonathan Carver, the early British trader who visited here after the War of 1812. Whoever named them was apparently under the misconception that there were only 12 islands and named the group in honor of the Apostles of Jesus. The Indians had their own descriptive names for the islands–Willow Tree, Maple Sugar, Burnt Wood, Red Stone–but most of these have been changed. The French, too, had their own names. Stockton Island, for example, was Presque Isle.

Henry Schoolcraft, who accompanied the Cass expedition of 1820 to explore Lake Superior country, named the Apostles the Federation Islands and gave each individual island the name of a state. Michigan and York Islands remain of the names he selected. Present names of some of the islands also reveal something about their geography–North Twin, Rocky and Outer Islands are a few examples. The island that Schoolcraft named Minnesota has been called Hermit Island since 1861 when its sole occupant, Thomas Wilson, died. He lived there in solitude from 1847-1861 because, it is said, he was disappointed in love. Others say that his self-imposed exile suited Wilson's generally quarrelsome nature.

With the development of Bayfield as a port for handling lumber, fish and brownstone, lighthouses went up on some of the Apostle Islands to guide ships safely among them. The first lighthouse was built on Michigan Island in 1857 to guide ships through the passage between Michigan and Stockton Islands; it was rebuilt at the south end of the island in 1930. The next light was built on Raspberry Island in 1863 and a fog signal added in 1903. Lights were also placed on Outer, Sand and Devil's Islands. The lighthouse on Devil's Island is

A small fishing village on Willy's Island, one of the Apostles.

Apostle Islands mailman used a dog sled to cross the winter ice to Bayfield, circa 1875.

particularly important because of its isolated location at the outer perimeter of the islands. Three keepers man the light and also operate a communications station at the north end of the island. In 1978 all lighthouses on the Apostle Islands were completely automated.

Although lumbering and quarrying were once carried out on some of the islands, logging operations ended on Stockton Island in 1918 and the brownstone quarries on Basswood Island have been closed since 1900. The National Lakeshore Park intends to use the quarry on Stockton Island to illustrate this once-important industry.

Winds and waves have carved caves into some of the rocky islands, most notably, Stockton and Devil's Islands. There are good swimming beaches on South

Twin, Ironwood and Raspberry Islands. Swimming in the bays of the islands is more enjoyable since the shallow protected waters are much warmer than the deeper water farther from shore.

Stockton Island also offers seven miles of maintained hiking trails and Rocky Island has a one and three-quarters mile trail near the ranger station.

La Pointe Indian burial ground.

110.   MADELINE ISLAND
AND BIG BAY STATE PARK

The Chippewa Indians referred to this island as the "Isle of the golden-breasted woodpecker," their name for the flicker once found in great numbers here. Father Claude Allouez, a Jesuit priest, began a mission on the island in 1663, calling it La Point du Saint Esprit. Allouez was transferred to Sault Ste. Marie in 1668, but his presence brought the island to the attention of the French. They built a fort here in 1693 to protect their fur trade. It was abandoned five years later when the fur trade fell off. The North West Company made the island a busy trading center in 1791 and brought John Johnston and Michel Cadotte to the island as agents. Cadotte married Chief White Crane's daughter, Equaysayway (Traveling Woman), but Cadotte gave her the Christian name of Madeline--the name by which the island is known today.

When the American Fur Company took over the island in 1834, it began a fishing center. The following year, the Rev. Sherman Hall opened the first Protestant mission here. Father Frederic Baraga made his way to the island in 1836 and established a Roman Catholic Mission and a cemetery. The La Pointe Cemetery, burying place for both Indian and white settlers, and located near the log Catholic Church, has been nominated for inclusion on the National Register of Historic Places. Two of those buried here are Michel Cadotte, who died in 1837, and Chief Buffalo, chief of the Chippewa at the time of the signing of the La Pointe treaty of 1854. Chief Buffalo was born on the island around 1759. Just a few months before his death he had returned from a trip to Washington to confer with President Franklin Pierce about treaty matters. While he was there, the sculptor Francis Vincent executed a marble bust of this remarkable man, which may be seen today in the U.S. Senate Gallery.

Madeline Island may be reached by ferry from Bayfield except during three months of the year when Lake Superior freezes. Then automobiles can be driven across the ice to the island.

Madeline Island Historical Museum.

In summer, a bus takes the island visitor on a conducted tour of natural and historic highlights of Madeline Island. The one and one-quarter hour tour leaves the La Pointe dock several times during the afternoon in summer. ($)

Madeline Island Historical Museum, now affiliated with the State Historical Society of Wisconsin, was begun in 1958 by Mr. and Mrs. Leo Capser, who had been summer residents on the island since 1903. The museum is housed in four buildings, which have been joined together, with the outer wall of one building becoming the inner wall of another. The buildings, which display early craftsmanship, originally functioned as the town jail, a log barn, an agency of the American Fur Company and a home for distressed sailors. The stockade that surrounds the museum was built by local craftsmen from hand-hewn logs.

Big Bay State Park, (P-H-C-F-S). On the southeastern shore of Madeline Island is Big Bay, from which this state park takes its name. A beach across the mouth of Big Bay has formed Big Bay Lagoon. A marshland wildlife refuge surrounds the lagoon. Big Bay State Park was formerly the site of a lumber camp. There are one and one-half miles of swimming beach in the park and two miles of hiking trails. Capacity crowds use the campsites in summer.

La Pointe Lighthouse*, built in 1858, is situated on Long Island, south of Madeline Island.

(Numbered entries continued on p. 162)

Eastman Johnson's charcoal drawing of Ken Ne Waw Be Mint, a Chippewa.

THE CHIPPEWA PEOPLE OF LAKE SUPERIOR

Of all the Indian people of Lake Superior, the Chippewa have figured most prominently in the recorded history of the region. Three names—Chippewa, Ojibway and Ojibwa—are used to refer to the same tribe, which dates from the seventeenth century in the Lake Superior area. The two names most frequently used today are Chippewa, thought to be an English corruption of Ojibwa; and Ojibwa which means "to roast until puckered," referring to puckered moccasin seams. The American Bureau of Ethnology adopted the designation Chippewa (used in this book) early in this century, reflecting the wishes of many tribal members. Today younger tribal members prefer the term Ojibwa, now used almost exclusively in Canada. Both Chippewa and Ojibwa are used in the United States.

According to anthropologists, the Chippewa Indians were part of a very large migration of Indians from the East into the Sault Ste. Marie-Mackinac area in the seventeenth century. From there, the Chippewa pressed west around the shores of Lake Superior, into northern Minnesota, North Dakota and southern Manitoba. Extremely courageous and successful warriors, the Chippewa had little trouble expanding their territory in the Lake Superior-Lake Huron area. They managed to drive the Sioux across the Mississippi and beyond, until Chippewa territory spread as far west as the headwaters of the Red River, located in what is now western Minnesota and North Dakota. They were in constant conflict with the Fox tribe and eventually drove that tribe out of northern Wisconsin with the help of the French.

With the French, however, the Chippewa were uniformly friendly. They engaged in fur trade first with the French and later, after the fall of New France, with the British and Americans. Until the close of the War of 1812, they resisted the westward tide of white settlement and provided a real challenge to Catholic and Protestant missionaries who found their native religion deeply-ingrained. The Medewiwin, a tribal medicine society, exerted much influence and for many decades dictated the migrations of the tribe.

Under pressure from American and Canadian settlers, the Chippewa gradually gave up their native hunting grounds during the nineteenth century. By treaties, the Canadian and American governments gathered them together on reservations. With the exception of two small bands that moved west, the Chippewa were settled in the Superior-Huron area by the U.S. government.

Romanticized memories of Chippewa life in past centuries live on in the minds of many Americans who have read Henry Wadsworth Longfellow's famous poem, "Song of Hiawatha." The character Hiawatha is a Victorian version of the legendary Chippewa hero, Nanabazhoo. Part of the Chippewa cultural legacy lives on in legends collected from 1903-1905 by William Jones and published by the American Ethnological Society. The legends make delightful reading, particularly the ones relating to Nanabazhoo. Historian Grace Lee Nute characterized him as the "combined Messiah, Puck, Prometheus and Loki of the Chippewa." He was their aid and protector, who brought them fire and discovered tobacco. He is the Sleeping Giant at Thunder Bay (see entry 26).

Chippewa legends also offer delightful explanations for the shape of land forms, the origin and physical appearance of the animals of the area and the behavior of the weather and the lake. Travelers will hear of these legends from time to time as they tour around the lake-shore. One such Chippewa legend attributes the origin of Lake Superior whitefish to a domestic tragedy. An Indian husband found his wife guilty of infidelity and murdered her. Her spirit returned to haunt her two children who ran away to escape it. She chased them to the St. Mary's River, where a crane gathered up all three to ferry them over the river. During the crossing, the mother fell into the rapids where she was transformed into the whitefish, a very important fish to the Indians of the Sault.

Another example of the Chippewa culture can be found along the shores of Lake Superior —picture writing or pictographs. Some of the drawings include moose, deer, Indian war-riors, homes, and canoes. These can be found in 28 different locations in the Quetico Provincial Park, the Superior National Forest in Minnesota (lying to the south of the Quetico) and in Lake Superior Provincial Park. Nineteenth century travelers also reported picture writing at the northern edge of the lake near Schreiber and St. Ignace Island (Les Ecrits and Les Petits Ecrits), at Thunder Cape and Pigeon Point. They also reported carv-ings on sandstone rock near Bad River. Henry Schoolcraft, the famous U.S. Indian agent at Sault Ste. Marie who recorded so much about the ways of Chippewa life for posterity, interpreted a few of these Indian paintings but the meaning of many others is lost.

Today, there are nine Chippewa Indian Reservations scattered around the Canadian north shore of Lake Superior—at or near Thunder Bay, Rossport, Marathon, White Lake Pro-vincial Park, Michipicoten, Wawa, Goulais River, Gros Cap and Garden River. Another six reservations lie along the American shore at Bay Mills, Keweenaw Bay, Bad River, Red Cliff, Fond du Lac and Grand Portage.

Chippewa Indians, circa 1900.

All these reservations are unpleasant social testimony to the changes forced upon the Chippewa by the coming of the white man. Once seminomadic, forest-dwelling hunters, fishermen and wild rice gatherers, the Chippewa ranged over hundreds of thousands of square miles of northern Great Lakes forests. They lived in dome-shaped wigwams covered with birch bark and grass mats and were experts with the birchbark canoe. Today, theirs is a relatively sedentary way of life, either on or off the reservations. They are among the largest remnants of the aboriginal population in North America; approximately 80,000 live on reservation lands in the United States and Canada. An even larger number live off the reservations where they engage in a wide variety of occupations, among them agriculture, arts, education, law and medicine. A good place to visit the Chippewa people is at Assinins, the site of the Father Baraga mission, established in 1843 and now the Keweenaw Bay Tribal Center (see entry 77).

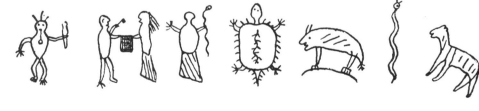

Birch bark record from White Earth, Minnesota.

111. RED CLIFF RESERVATION

[Hy 13]

About 550 Chippewa Indians live on or adjacent to this 7,267-acre reservation, which was created from land given the Red Cliff Band of the Chippewa by the terms of the Treaty of La Pointe in 1854.

On the reservation, the traveler can visit a community center building and a Catholic mission that has served the Red Cliff Band since frontier times. Medicine dances, important community events, are held there semiannually. At Red Cliff and Raspberry Bay, tribally-operated campgrounds offer facilities for the public. The Red Cliff Point Detour campground, with 30 campsites, lies one-half mile east of the National Lakeshore on land donated by Red Cliff Reservation. This campsite was made possible through a federal grant and the donation of timber by Red Cliff Reservation. Campers will enjoy both excellent fishing and boating on Lake Superior shoreland. There is also a fishing guide service and a boat ramp. An Indian Arts and Crafts Center is open daily. ($—senior citizens admitted free.)

Red Cliff Indian pageant, 1924.

Sevona Cottage on Sand Island, 1915.

112. SAND ISLAND

[Westernmost of the Apostle Islands]

A sandy shoal connects Sand Island and Little Sand Bay. The first settler on Sand Island was Francis Shaw, a Civil War veteran, who received land on the island as a veteran's bonus. This became the nucleus of a permanent settlement of year-round fishermen/farmers. Buildings that were once part of the Shaw Farm* and the dock still stand.

In the 1880s, Samuel Fifield, editor of the *Ashland Weekly Press*, made the island a popular summer resort when he began a tent colony there. Fifield, who thought Sand Island a "miniature paradise," salvaged hatch covers from the ore carrier SEVONA, wrecked off the island in 1903. With these, he built Sevona Cottage,* which he occupied during the summer. He traveled between the island and the mainland in his palatial yacht, STELLA.

The Sand Island Lighthouse, built in 1881 of sandstone quarried on the island, is equipped with an automatic light today. Many consider the old lighthouse an important historic landmark along with the Sand Island school, built about 1910 and closed in the 1930s.

On Little Sand Bay, across from the island on the mainland, the Hokenson brothers built a fishing dock in 1927. Today the three picturesque buildings and the dock* house the only fishing and packing operation within the Apostle Islands National Lakeshore Park, even though fishing was once a very important industry in the area.

113.   SOUTH SHORE DRIVE BETWEEN BAYFIELD AND SUPERIOR

[Hy 13]

Cornucopia was named by a Minneapolis lawyer, T. J. Stevenson, who founded the community in 1902 expecting it to become a depot stop on the

Cornucopia fishing boats in winter dry dock.

Port Wing School was Wisconsin's first consolidated school. Wagons and sleds provided the first free "bussing" in the state.

railroad. The route of the railroad, however, took it elsewhere and its accompanying bounty never reached Cornucopia. The community was forced to rely, instead, on the surrounding forests and on the lake at its door for a livelihood.

Two sawmills and nine lumber camps attracted a number of Slavic immigrants, who built St. Mary's Russian Orthodox Church with its two octagonal towers. Today, the church still has a congregation of about ten families. Other settlers came from the Door County area to begin a small fishing colony here. Now lumbering has ended and commercial fishing activity has been greatly reduced. The scenery, however, remains unblemished and the traveler will find the falls of the Sisikiwit River on Town Line Road, one-half mile east of the village, well worth seeing. The falls, six to eight feet high, drop over limestone cliffs as the river empties into the vast depths of Lake Superior.

Port Wing, a small fishing village on the south shore, formed the state's first consolidated school district in 1903. Because the students were mainly loggers' children who lived many miles from the school, a canvas-covered horse sleigh picked them up daily--the first tax-supported transportation system provided by an educational district in Wisconsin.

Twin Falls Park, at the junction of Hys 13 and A, has a campground and a trail leading to two graceful waterfalls.

Brule River, crossed by Hy 13, served as one of the most traveled routes of the voyageurs. The river links Lake Superior with the St. Croix and Mississippi Rivers. One of the few wild rivers in Wisconsin, the Brule ranks among the nation's best trout streams.

Davidson Mill on Hy 13, 12-1/2 miles east of Superior in the Amnicon River Valley. Jacob Tapola, a Finnish immigrant, built this feed mill in 1900. Tapola, who worked two years to complete the mill, carved the gears by hand and got the millstones from the riverbed. Tapola designed the mill with eight wings in the Finnish style unlike the Dutch windmills that have only four. Eugene Davidson, Tapola's grandson, owns the mill today.

Davidson Feed Mill.

Bibliography

General

Boyer, Dwight. *Great Stories of the Great Lakes.* Dodd Mead and Co., New York, 1966.

Boyer, Dwight. *True Tales of the Great Lakes.* Dodd Mead and Co., New York, 1971.

Hatcher, Harlan H., and Walter, Erich A. *A Pictorial History of the Great Lakes.* Crown Publishers, New York, 1963.

Havighurst, Walter, editor. *The Great Lakes Reader.* Macmillan Co., New York, 1966.

Karlan, Arno, editor, and Steinhaker, Charles, photographer. *Superior: Portrait of a Living Lake,* second ed. Harper and Row, New York, 1970.

Nute, Grace Lee. *Lake Superior.* Bobbs-Merrill Co., New York, 1944.

Books with a Geographic Focus

Arthur, Elizabeth. *The Thunder Bay District, 1821-1892.* The Champlain Society, Toronto, 1973.

Bayliss, Joseph E. and Estelle L., and Quaife, Milo M. *River of Destiny, The Saint Mary's.* Wayne University Press, Detroit, 1955.

Blegen, Theodore C. *Minnesota, A History of the State.* University of Minnesota Press, Minneapolis, 1963.

Dunbar, Willis Frederick. *Michigan: A History of the Wolverine State.* Eerdmans Publishing Co., Grand Rapids, 1965.

May, George S. *Pictorial History of Michigan,* 2 vols. Eerdmans Publishing Co., Grand Rapids, 1967, 1969.

McInnis, Edgar. *Canada, A Political and Social History,* third ed. Holt, Rinehart and Winston, Toronto, 1969.

Napoli, James. *The Coasts of Wisconsin.* University of Wisconsin Sea Grant College Program, Madison, 1975.

Nesbitt, Robert C. *Wisconsin, A History.* University of Wisconsin Press, Madison, 1973.

Purinton, James. *Wisconsin Coastal History Trails: Lake Superior.* Wisconsin Coastal Zone Management Development Program, Madison, 1976.

Smith, Alice E. Vol. I of *The History of Wisconsin: From Exploration to Statehood.* State Historical Society of Wisconsin, Madison, 1973.

The Indians

Densmore, Frances. *Chippewa Customs.* U.S. Government Printing Office, Washington, D.C., 1929.

Dewdney, Selwyn, and Kidd, Kenneth E. *Indian Rock Paintings of the Great Lakes,* second ed. University of Toronto Press, 1967.

Jones, William. *Ojibwa Texts:* Vol. 1 *Nanabushu Tales* and Vol. II *Miscellaneous Tales.* G. E. Stechert and Co., New York, agents for E. J. Brill, Ltd., Leyden, Netherlands, 1917, 1919.

Quimby, George I. *Indian Life in the Upper Great Lakes, 1000 B.C. to A.D. 1800.* University of Chicago Press, 1960.

Geology

Hough, Jack L. *Geology of the Great Lakes.* University of Illinois Press, Urbana, 1958.

Mapping

Karpinski, Louis C. *Historical Atlas of the Great Lakes and Michigan*. Michigan Historical Commission, Lansing, 1931.

Exploration and Travel

Agassiz, Louis. *Lake Superior . . . with a Narrative of the Tour by J. Elliot Cabot*. Arno Press Reprint, New York, 1970.

Brebner, John B. *The Explorers of North America, 1492-1806*. The Macmillan Co., New York, 1933.

Nute, Grace L. *Caesars of the Wilderness: Médard Chouart, Sieur des Groseilliers and Pierre Esprit Radisson, 1618-1710*. Bobbs-Merrill Co., New York, 1944.

Schoolcraft, Henry. *Narrative of Travels . . . to the Sources of the Mississippi River in the Year 1820*. Arno Press Reprint, New York, 1970.

French and British

Kellogg, Louise P. *The British Regime in Wisconsin and the Northwest*. State Historical Society of Wisconsin, Madison, 1935.

Wrong, George M. *The Rise and Fall of New France*. The Macmillan Co., New York, 1928.

Fur Trade

Campbell, Marjorie Wilkins. *The North West Company*. St. Martin's Press, New York, 1957.

Innis, Harold A. *The Fur Trade in Canada: An Introduction to Canadian Economic History*. Yale University Press, New Haven, 1930.

Morse, Eric W. *Fur Trade Canoe Routes of Canada – Then and Now*. Queens Printer, Ottawa, 1969.

Nute, Grace L. *The Voyageur*. D. Appleton and Co., New York, 1931.

Phillips, Paul C. *The Fur Trade*, 2 vols. University of Oklahoma Press, Norman, 1961.

Quimby, George I. *Indian Culture and European Trade Goods*. University of Wisconsin Press, Madison, 1966.

Rich, Edwin E. *The History of the Hudson's Bay Company, 1670-1870*. 2 vols. Hudson's Bay Record Society, London, 1958-1959.

Missionaries

Clark, James I. *Father Claude Allouez, Missionary*. State Historical Society of Wisconsin, Madison, 1957.

Goodykoontz, Colin B. *Home Missions on the American Frontier*. The Caxton Printers, Caldwell, Id., 1939.

Jamison, James K. *By Cross and Anchor: The Story of Frederic Baraga on Lake Superior*. St. Anthony Guild Press, Paterson, N.J., 1946.

Kennedy, John H. *Jesuit and Savage in New France*. Yale University Press, New Haven, 1950.

Kenton, Edna, editor. *Black Gown and Redskins: Adventures and Travels of the Early Jesuit Missionaries in North America*. Longmans, New York, 1956.

Boats and Ships

Bowen, Dana Thomas. *Shipwrecks of the Lakes*. (private printing) Daytona Beach, 1952.

Kuttruff, Karl, and Glick, David B. *Ships of the Great Lakes: A Pictorial History*. Wayne State University Press, Detroit, 1976.

Ratigan, William. *Great Lakes Shipwrecks and Survivals*. Eerdmans, Grand Rapids, Mich., 1977.

Copper Mining

Benedict, C. Harry. *Red Metal: The Calumet and Hecla Story*. University of Michigan Press, Ann Arbor, 1952.

Gates, William B. *Michigan Copper and Boston Dollars*. Harvard University Press, Cambridge, Mass., 1951.

Rintala, Edsel K. *Douglass Houghton, Michigan's Pioneer Geologist*. Wayne State University Press, Detroit, 1954.

Iron Mining

Boyum, Burton H. *The Saga of Iron Mining in Michigan's Upper Peninsula.* Marquette County Historical Society, Marquette, Mich., 1977.

Hatcher, Harlan. *A Century of Iron and Men.* Bobbs-Merrill, Indianapolis, 1950.

Lafayette, Kenneth D. *Flaming Brands: Fifty Years of Iron-Making in the Upper Peninsula of Michigan, 1849-1898.* Northern Michigan University Press, Marquette, 1977.

Walker, David. *Discovery and Exploitation of Iron Ore Resources in Northeastern Minnesota: The Formative Years, 1865-1901.* 1973 doctoral dissertation, University of Wisconsin, to be published by the Minnesota Historical Society Press in 1979.

Lumbering

Fries, Robert F. *Empire in Pine: The Story of Lumbering in Wisconsin, 1830-1900.* State Historical Society of Wisconsin, Madison, 1951.

Gates, Paul W. *The Wisconsin Pine Lands of Cornell University.* Cornell University Press, Ithaca, N.Y., 1943.

Hidy, Ralph W. *Timber and Men, the Weyerhaeuser Story.* Macmillan, New York, 1963.

Larson, Agnes M. *History of the White Pine Industry in Minnesota.* University of Minnesota Press, Minneapolis, 1949.

Maybee, Rolland H. *Michigan's White Pine Era, 1840-1900.* Michigan Historical Commission, Lansing, 1960.

Wyman, Walker. *Mythical Creatures of the North Country.* River Falls State University Press, River Falls, Wis., 1969.

Fishing

Downs, Warren. *Fish of Lake Superior.* University of Wisconsin Sea Grant College Program, Madison, 1976.

"The North Shore, Lake Superior," first published in 1892 in *Harper's New Monthly Magazine.*

Index

Credits

PHOTOS

Allan Bogue, 5, 36, 38, 46, 49, 112, 116, 120, 123, 129, 130; State Historical Society of Wisconsin, 6, 8, 13, 21, 22-23, 30, 37, 48, 52, 57, 61, 62, 71, 73, 76, 80, 84, 86, 100, 110, 113, 115, 119, 124-125, 135, 137, 139, 140-141, 143, 144, 146, 147, 150-151, 152-153, 155, 156, 157, 158, 160-161, 161, 163, 168; Douglas County Historical Museum, 10; Duluth Public Public Library, 11, 17, 19; Seaway Port Authority, 12; Peyton Smith, 18, 82; Bruce Ojard, 20; Lake Carriers Association, 24; Minnesota Historical Society, 26, 27, 31, 98-99; Minnesota Department of Economic Development, 29, 33; Minnesota Department of Natural Resources, 32; Glenbow Alberta Institute, 35, front cover; National Park Service, 40, 154; Ryck Lydecker, 41, 108, 179; Ontario Ministry of Natural Resources, 42, 53, 54, 55, 58, 59; Metropolitan Toronto Library, 44; Ontario Ministry of Industry and Tourism, 45, 60, 63, 74; U. S. Forest Service, 50; Detroit District, Army Corps of Engineers, 70, 81; Sault Daily Star, 77; Michigan Department of State Archives, 79, 92, 117, 126-127, 128; Linda Weimer, 15, 87, 90, 95, 104, 132, 149; Alger County Historical Society, 88, 89; U. S. Coast Guard, 91; Marquette County Historical Society, 93; Marquette and Huron Mountain Railroad, 94; Immigration History Research Center, University of Minnesota, 96-97, 118; Wisconsin Department of Natural Resources, 101; L'Anse Sentinel, 102; Margaret Bogue, 65, 68, 103, 106-107; Michigan Travel Commission, 105, 133, 134; Michigan Technological University Library, 111, 122; Houghton County Historical Museum, 114; Hurley Courthouse, 136; Farm Security Administration, 142; William H. Tishler, 148; St. Louis County Historical Society, Duluth, Minn., 159; Bayfield County Historical Society, 162, 165; Jean Lang, 164; Linda Paulson, 179.

MAPS

Jana Fothergill, 14, 16, 47, 75, 78.

Eric W. Morse, *Fur Trade Canoe Routes of Canada - Then and Now*, Ottawa, 1969. Courtesy of the Department of Indian and Northern Affairs of Canada, 39.

Adapted with permission from a map prepared for the State Historical Society of Wisconsin, 64.

State Historical Society of Wisconsin, 2, 66-67.

Adapted from Michael D. McNamara, *Metallic Mining in the Lake Superior Region: Perspectives and Projections.* University of Wisconsin-Madison Institute for Environmental Studies, 1976, 98, 127.

The University of Wisconsin Cartography Laboratory produced the large map of Lake Superior (pocket of inside back cover).

"Farewell, Lake Superior! We have shaken hands and parted in peace."

—Charles W. Penny, 1840

For additional copies, contact:

Sea Grant Communications Office
University of Wisconsin
1800 University Avenue
Madison, WI 53706

or

The University of Wisconsin Press
114 North Murray Street
Madison, WI 53715

Trip Record